PRAISE FOR STACK HAPPY

"Oh my gosh! How can you not love this cookbook? I've been such a fan of Karly's blog, *Buns in My Oven*, for a number of years now. Karly is enormously talented, and I want to make every single one of her recipes! This book is filled with such creative and drool-worthy flapjacks. I can hardly wait to make them for my family!"

—*Lori Lange*, author of *The Recipe Girl Cookbook* and founder of RecipeGirl.com

STACK HAPPY

70 FLIPPING DELICIOUS FLAPJACK RECIPES
for breakfast, dinner, and dessert

KARLY CAMPBELL

Front Table Books ❖ An imprint of Cedar Fort, Inc. ❖ Springville, Utah

ISBN: 978-1-4621-1537-2

Published by Front Table Books, an imprint of Cedar Fort, Inc.
2373 W. 700 S., Springville, UT, 84663
Distributed by Cedar Fort, Inc., www.cedarfort.com

LIBRARY OF CONGRESS CATALOGING-IN-PUBLICATION DATA

Campbell, Karly, 1982- author
Stack happy : 70 flipping delicious flapjack recipes for breakfast, dinner, and dessert / Karly Campbell.
    pages cm
Includes index.
ISBN 978-1-4621-1537-2 (acid-free paper)
1. Pancakes, waffles, etc. I. Title.
TX770.P34C36 2015
641.81'53--dc23
                                    2014034845

Cover and page design by Bekah Claussen and Lauren Error
Cover design © 2015 by Lyle Mortimer
Edited by Justin Greer and Bekah Claussen

Printed in China

10 9 8 7 6 5 4 3 2 1

Printed on acid-free paper

CONTENTS

viii INTRODUCTION

1 FRUITY FUN

26 BREAKFAST WITH A TWIST

50 HEALTHIER PANCAKES

80 SAVORY PANCAKES

108 DESSERT PANCAKES

136 SAUCES AND SYRUPS

167 INDEX

169 ABOUT THE AUTHOR

170 ACKNOWLEDGMENTS

INTRODUCTION

Is it true that every family has one? A pancake maker, I mean. I hope so.

In my family, the pancake maker is my dad. When I was little, he'd make them for us on the weekends. Now that I'm grown with children of my own, he makes them for his grandkids when they sleep over. He's a darn good pancake maker too. Of course, his secret recipe is a box mix and replacing the water or milk with heavy cream. I said he was a good pancake maker, not a pancake maker on a diet.

My mama always told me that I would grow up to be an author. I more or less assumed she was nuts and rolled my eyes whenever she said that. It makes me happy that I have, in fact, grown up to be an author, and that my first book is full of pancake recipes. It seems like the perfect way to honor the two people who helped me become the person I am today.

Before I get too syrupy sweet (see what I did there?), I'll just stop while I'm ahead. I've poured my heart and soul into this book and these recipes, and I hope you'll enjoy them as much as my family has enjoyed playing taste tester.

Pancakes are a long-standing Saturday morning tradition for so many, and I really hope that this book will help you enjoy that family time even more, preferably while covered in sticky maple syrup with happy smiles and requests for seconds or thirds.

My other hope for this book is that you view pancakes, which I consider one of life's greatest pleasures, as more than just a quick breakfast option or something to be topped only with butter and maple syrup. I've included an entire chapter of dessert pancakes. After all, a pancake is basically a cake that's cooked on the stove, right? Sounds like dessert to me! I've also included a chapter full of savory dinner recipes. Kids love pancakes, and serving them up for dinner is always a win in my house. Even the breakfast pancakes are very creative, so you don't have to settle for the same stack twice.

Enjoy!

TIPS & TECHNIQUES

Buttermilk

I know, I know. Buttermilk isn't something that I always have on hand, either. Why, then, does nearly every recipe in this book call for it? Because it's the best. Truly.

If a pancake craving hits and you're out of buttermilk, you can do one of two things.

Buttermilk powder is usually available in the baking aisle and lasts for quite some time. You'll just add the powder to the dry ingredients and replace the buttermilk in the recipe with water.

Another option, and the one I usually go for, is to add two teaspoons of white vinegar to a measuring cup and then fill it with milk and let it sit for five minutes. I generally reduce the amount of liquid in a recipe by ¼ cup when doing this. If the recipe calls for one cup of buttermilk, I would use only ¾ of a cup of this replacement. If you use the full cup, your batter will be a bit thinner and your pancakes won't puff up quite as much.

Oil or Butter?

Just about every recipe in this book calls for a couple table-spoons of vegetable oil added to the wet ingredients. Melted butter makes a great substitute for the oil if you're in a pinch or prefer to cook with butter instead of oil.

Overmixing

Every pancake recipe out there mentions stirring just until the ingredients are combined—and with good reason! Over-mixing will lead to tough pancakes. You want to stir gently, with a wire whisk or fork, until the ingredients are all moistened. You don't need to beat out every lump you come across. In fact, a few lumps are good! We want light and fluffy pancakes, not hockey pucks.

Swapping Flours

I tend to do most of my baking and cooking with all-purpose flour. Every now and then I'll use white whole wheat and sub that in with no other changes to a recipe. If you'd like to swap in whole wheat flour for all-purpose flour, I suggest subbing whole wheat for half of the flour and leaving the other half white, at least the first time you make the recipe. This will help you to judge whether or not you need to add more liquid to the recipe. If the recipe is too dry, just bump up the liquid a bit the next time you make it.

Thick Batters

You'll notice that most of the recipes in this book produce a much thicker batter than you're probably used to, especially if you usually make pancakes from a box. This is because I enjoy big, puffy pancakes, and I believe a thick batter helps. I use a ¼-cup dry measure to scoop out batter and pour onto the griddle. If the batter is very thick, I'll use the bottom of the measure to gently swirl it around a bit, just to lightly spread it out.

Equipment

You can certainly get by with no special equipment, but I really prefer cooking my pancakes on an electric griddle. Mine is just a cheap griddle from the local big box store, but it works brilliantly. I can cook an entire batch of pancakes in one go, and everyone eats at the same time.

If you're cooking your pancakes in a skillet on the stove, keep the oven set to warm and place a cookie sheet on the middle rack. Place the pancakes on the cookie sheet as they come out of the skillet to keep them warm until the whole batch is made.

FRUITY
fun

⚘♡⚘♡⚘♡⚘♡⚘♡⚘♡⚘♡⚘

Fruit is always a good choice for the breakfast table, and this chapter will help you get creative in that department! From Blueberry Granola Pancakes to pancakes with all of Elvis's favorite flavors, this chapter has something for every fruit lover.

⚘♡⚘♡⚘♡⚘♡⚘♡⚘♡⚘♡⚘♡⚘

PEACH PECAN PANCAKES

I believe, deep in my heart, that I'm a true Southern belle. Of course, I grew up in the Midwest and don't know the first thing about the proper way to make sweet tea, so it's clearly all in my head. But, that doesn't mean that my first bite of these sweet peach pancakes didn't get my Southern accent kick-started. Slightly sweet, with a bit of crunch from the pecans, these pancakes will make your morning a little happier.

Prep Time: 10 minutes
Cook Time: 10 minutes
Total Time: 20 minutes
Yield: 8 (4-inch) pancakes

For the pancakes:
1 cup flour
2 Tbsp. brown sugar
1 tsp. ground cinnamon
1 tsp. baking powder
½ tsp. baking soda
½ tsp. salt
⅔ cup buttermilk
½ cup peach purée
1 egg, beaten
2 Tbsp. vegetable oil
1 tsp. vanilla extract

For the topping:
½ cup diced peaches (fresh or canned)
¼ cup chopped pecans
maple syrup

Heat a large skillet or griddle over medium heat.

In a medium bowl, combine the flour, sugar, cinnamon, baking powder, baking soda, and salt. Whisk to combine.

In a small bowl, mix together the buttermilk, peach purée, egg, oil, and vanilla.

Stir the wet ingredients into the dry ingredients until combined but still slightly lumpy.

Spray your cooking surface with nonstick cooking spray and pour ¼ cup of the pancake batter in the pan. Cook for 3 minutes per side or until cooked through. Repeat with remaining pancakes.

Stack the pancakes, then top with diced peaches, pecans, and maple syrup before serving.

Note: For the peach purée, you can use a jar of baby food, so long as it's 100% peaches. Alternatively, place a peeled and pitted peach or canned, drained peaches in your blender and blend until puréed.

ELVIS PANCAKES

Have y'all heard of Elvis's favorite sandwich? A grilled peanut butter, banana, and bacon sandwich. Oh, yes. I went and made that into a pancake, and it's heavenly. The salty bacon, creamy peanut butter, and mashed bananas go perfectly together for breakfast!

Prep Time: 10 minutes
Cook Time: 10 minutes
Total Time: 20 minutes
Yield: 8 (4-inch) pancakes

1 cup flour
2 Tbsp. granulated sugar
1 tsp. baking powder
½ tsp. baking soda
½ tsp. salt
2 Tbsp. vegetable oil
1 cup buttermilk
1 egg, beaten
1 tsp. vanilla extract
2 ripe bananas
4 slices bacon, cooked and crumbled
½ cup peanut butter

Heat a large skillet or griddle over medium heat.

In a medium bowl, combine the flour, sugar, baking powder, baking soda, and salt. Whisk to combine.

In a small bowl, mix together the oil, buttermilk, egg, and vanilla. Use a fork to mash the bananas and stir into the wet mixture.

Stir the wet ingredients into the dry ingredients until combined but still slightly lumpy.

Spray your cooking surface with nonstick cooking spray and pour ¼ cup of the pancake batter in the pan. Sprinkle a few bacon crumbles over the wet batter. When bubbles form and pop, flip the pancake and continue cooking until golden brown and cooked through. Repeat with remaining pancakes.

Warm the peanut butter in a microwave-safe dish and spoon over the pancakes before serving.

APPLE CIDER PANCAKES WITH APPLE CIDER SYRUP

Our family looks forward to our annual trip to the apple orchard every fall. The best part? The little sample-sized cups of apple cider. We love taste testing the cider and bringing gallons home to enjoy for later! I added a bit of our apple cider to these pancakes and topped it with a cider syrup that really brings out the flavors of fall!

Prep Time: 5 minutes
Cook Time: 10 minutes
Total Time: 15 minutes
Yield: 8 (4-inch) pancakes

1 cup flour
1 Tbsp. sugar
1 tsp. baking powder
½ tsp. baking soda
¼ tsp. salt
¼ tsp. cinnamon
½ cup apple cider
¼ cup buttermilk
¼ cup Greek yogurt
1 egg, beaten
2 Tbsp. oil
Apple Cider Syrup, page 152

Heat a large skillet or griddle over medium heat.

In a medium bowl, combine the flour, sugar, baking powder, baking soda, salt, and cinnamon. Whisk to combine.

In a small bowl, mix together the apple cider, buttermilk, Greek yogurt, egg, and oil.

Stir the wet ingredients into the dry ingredients until combined but still slightly lumpy.

Spray your cooking surface with nonstick cooking spray and pour ¼ cup of the pancake batter in the pan. When bubbles form and pop, flip the pancake and continue cooking until golden brown and cooked through. Repeat with remaining pancakes.

Drizzle generously with Apple Cider Syrup.

Note: If you don't have any apple cider on hand, apple juice works just as well.

BLUEBERRY GRANOLA CRUNCH PANCAKES

I'm a big fan of crunchy granola, and it just pairs so well with juicy blueberries. Mixing it into the pancake batter adds a delightful, hearty texture to your breakfast that's complemented nicely with the berries. Don't forget to drown everything in warm maple syrup before devouring!

Prep Time: 5 minutes
Cook Time: 10 minutes
Total Time: 15 minutes
Yield: 8 (4-inch) pancakes

1 cup flour
1 Tbsp. sugar
1 tsp. baking powder
½ tsp. baking soda
½ tsp. ground cinnamon
¼ tsp. salt
1 cup buttermilk
1 egg, beaten
2 Tbsp. vegetable oil
1 tsp. vanilla extract
½ cup granola
1 cup blueberries, rinsed and dried

Heat a large skillet or griddle over medium heat.

In a medium bowl, combine the flour, sugar, baking powder, baking soda, cinnamon, and salt and whisk to combine.

In a small bowl, mix together the buttermilk, egg, oil, and vanilla.

Stir the wet ingredients into the dry ingredients until combined but still slightly lumpy. Gently stir in the granola.

Spray your cooking surface with nonstick cooking spray and pour ¼ cup of the pancake batter in the pan. Sprinkle a few berries on the pancake and use the back of a spoon or your finger to lightly cover the berries with extra pancake batter. Cook for 3 minutes per side or until cooked through. Repeat with remaining pancakes.

Serve topped with extra granola, blueberries, and warm maple syrup.

PUMPKIN PANCAKES WITH BROWNED BUTTER DRIZZLE

I don't know about you, but my pantry is never without a can or two of pumpkin. I don't care what time of year it is—sometimes you just need a slice of pumpkin pie or a stack of pumpkin pancakes! These pancakes are super moist, full of pumpkin flavor, and the browned butter drizzle is good enough to drink. Not that I would ever do such a thing. (I totally would.)

Prep Time: 10 minutes
Cook Time: 10 minutes
Total Time: 20 minutes
Yield: 8 (4-inch) pancakes

1 cup flour
2 Tbsp. brown sugar
1 tsp. ground cinnamon
1 tsp. baking powder
½ tsp. baking soda
½ tsp. salt
¼ tsp. nutmeg
2 Tbsp. vegetable oil
¾ cup buttermilk
1 tsp. vanilla extract
1 egg, beaten
½ cup pumpkin purée
Browned Butter Drizzle, page 140

Heat a large skillet or griddle over medium heat.

In a medium bowl, combine the flour, sugar, cinnamon, baking powder, baking soda, salt, and nutmeg. Whisk to combine.

In a small bowl, mix together the oil, buttermilk, vanilla, egg, and pumpkin purée.

Stir the wet ingredients into the dry ingredients until combined but still slightly lumpy.

Spray your cooking surface with nonstick cooking spray and pour ¼ cup of the pancake batter in the pan. Cook for 3 minutes per side or until cooked through. Repeat with remaining pancakes.

Drizzle generously with Browned Butter Drizzle.

DOUBLE CHOCOLATE BANANA PANCAKES

Stack up these decadent, fudgy pancakes for a morning or afternoon treat that's loaded with bananas and drizzled with extra chocolate syrup for the perfect finishing touch. The bananas help make these pancakes extra moist and keep me from feeling too guilty about all of the chocolate.

Prep Time: 10 minutes
Cook Time: 10 minutes
Total Time: 20 minutes
Yield: 6 (4-inch) pancakes

1 cup flour
3 Tbsp. cocoa powder
2 Tbsp. granulated sugar
1 tsp. baking powder
½ tsp. baking soda
½ tsp. salt
⅔ cup buttermilk
2 Tbsp. vegetable oil
1 egg, beaten
1 tsp. vanilla extract
3 ripe bananas
¼ cup Chocolate Syrup, page 143
½ cup whipped cream

Heat a large skillet or griddle over medium heat.

In a medium bowl, combine the flour, cocoa powder, sugar, baking powder, baking soda, and salt. Whisk to combine.

In a small bowl, mix together the buttermilk, oil, egg, and vanilla. Use a fork to mash 2 of the bananas and stir into the wet mixture.

Stir the wet ingredients into the dry ingredients until combined but still slightly lumpy.

Spray your cooking surface with nonstick cooking spray and pour ¼ cup of the pancake batter in the pan. Cook for 3 minutes per side or until cooked through. Repeat with remaining pancakes.

Thinly slice the remaining banana. Serve over the pancakes with whipped cream and chocolate syrup.

DOUBLE CHOCOLATE BANANA PANCAKES

CARAMEL APPLE PANCAKES

Every kid I know adores apples, especially when served with caramel! I like the big, gooey caramel apples on a stick, and my kids like dipping slices in caramel sauce. No matter which way you enjoy your caramel apples, you'll love them on top of your pancakes!

Prep Time: 15 minutes
Cook Time: 15 minutes
Total Time: 30 minutes
Yield: 8 (4-inch) pancakes

For the pancakes:

1 cup flour
2 Tbsp. sugar
1 tsp. cinnamon
1 tsp. baking powder
½ tsp. baking soda
¼ tsp. salt
1 cup buttermilk
1 egg, beaten
2 Tbsp. vegetable oil
1 tsp. vanilla

For the apples:

2 Tbsp. butter
1 Tbsp. brown sugar
½ tsp. cinnamon
1 medium tart apple, peeled and diced
Salted Caramel Syrup, page 148

Heat a large skillet or griddle over medium heat.

In a medium bowl, combine the flour, sugar, cinnamon, baking powder, baking soda, and salt. Whisk to combine.

In a small bowl, mix together the buttermilk, egg, oil, and vanilla.

Stir the wet ingredients into the dry ingredients until combined but still slightly lumpy.

Spray your cooking surface with nonstick cooking spray and pour a ¼ cup of the pancake batter in the pan. Cook for 3 minutes per side or until cooked through. Repeat with remaining pancakes.

While the pancakes are cooking, set a small skillet over medium-low heat. Add the butter to the skillet and melt.

Stir in the brown sugar and cinnamon to combine.

Add the apples and stir to coat.

Cook for 5–7 minutes or until tender, stirring occasionally.

Top the pancakes with the warm apples and Salted Caramel Syrup.

RASPBERRY COOKIE BUTTER PANCAKES

Cookie butter is all the rage right now and with good reason! It can be found in most supermarkets near the peanut butter. Its creamy sweetness works so well with the tart raspberries—but I won't lie . . . I usually just eat my cookie butter with a spoon, while hiding in the pantry from my kids! No one wants to share their cookie butter. No one.

Prep Time: 10 minutes
Cook Time: 10 minutes
Total Time: 20 minutes
Yield: 6 (4-inch) pancakes

1 cup flour
2 Tbsp. granulated sugar
1 tsp. ground cinnamon
1 tsp. baking powder
½ tsp. baking soda
½ tsp. salt
¼ tsp. ground nutmeg
1 cup buttermilk
2 Tbsp. vegetable oil
1 egg, beaten
1 tsp. vanilla extract
½ cup fresh or frozen raspberries
¼ cup cookie butter

Heat a large skillet or griddle over medium heat.

In a medium bowl, combine the flour, sugar, cinnamon, baking powder, baking soda, salt, and nutmeg. Whisk to combine.

In a small bowl, mix together the buttermilk, egg, oil, and vanilla.

Stir the wet ingredients into the dry ingredients until combined but still slightly lumpy.

Spray your cooking surface with nonstick cooking spray and pour ¼ cup of the pancake batter in the pan. Gently press 3 or 4 raspberries into the pancake batter and use your finger or a spoon to spread a bit of batter over the berries.

Cook for 3 minutes per side or until cooked through. Repeat with remaining pancakes.

Heat the cookie butter in a microwave-safe dish for 15 seconds or until just melted enough to drizzle. Drizzle over the tops of the pancakes before serving.

CHOCOLATE STRAWBERRY SKEWERS

These bite-sized pancake skewers are a fun new take on the classic chocolate-covered strawberry. Pop 'em all on a cake stand at your next brunch for a delicious, bite-sized treat. I like to dip mine in whipped cream and chocolate syrup, but they're pretty tasty on their own too.

Prep Time: 10 minutes
Cook Time: 10 minutes
Total Time: 20 minutes
Yield: 30 skewers

1 cup flour
3 Tbsp. cocoa powder
2 Tbsp. sugar
1 tsp. baking powder
½ tsp. baking soda
¼ tsp. salt
1 cup, plus 2 Tbsp. buttermilk
1 egg, beaten
2 Tbsp. vegetable oil
1 tsp. vanilla extract
15 strawberries, hulled and sliced in half lengthwise
whipped cream, for serving
Chocolate Syrup, page 143

Heat a large skillet or griddle over medium heat.

In a medium bowl, combine the flour, cocoa powder, sugar, baking powder, baking soda, and salt. Whisk to combine.

In a small bowl, mix together the buttermilk, egg, oil, and vanilla.

Stir the wet ingredients into the dry ingredients until combined but still slightly lumpy.

Spray your cooking surface with nonstick cooking spray and drop 1 tablespoon of batter on the pan. Cook 1–2 minutes per side or until cooked through. Repeat to make 30 mini pancakes.

Place a half strawberry on each pancake and secure them with a toothpick.

Serve with fresh whipped cream and chocolate syrup.

CHOCOLATE STRAWBERRY SKEWERS

ORANGE VANILLA PANCAKES WITH VANILLA MAPLE SYRUP

I'm powerless when it comes to sweet, juicy oranges, so I knew I had to work them into some pancakes. These have a double punch of orange with a good portion of the liquid coming from (hopefully freshly squeezed!) orange juice and the addition of the orange zest.

Prep Time: 10 minutes
Cook Time: 10 minutes
Total Time: 20 minutes
Yield: 8 (4-inch) pancakes

For the pancakes:
1 cup flour
2 Tbsp. granulated sugar
1 tsp. baking powder
½ tsp. baking soda
½ tsp. salt
½ cup orange juice
¼ cup 2% milk
1 egg, beaten
2 Tbsp. vegetable oil
2 tsp. vanilla extract
1 Tbsp. orange zest

For the vanilla maple syrup:
½ cup maple syrup
2 tsp. vanilla extract

Heat a large skillet or griddle over medium heat.

In a medium bowl, combine the flour, sugar, baking powder, baking soda, and salt. Whisk to combine.

In a small bowl, mix together the orange juice, milk, egg, oil, vanilla, and orange zest.

Stir the wet ingredients into the dry ingredients until combined but still slightly lumpy.

Spray the cooking surface with nonstick cooking spray and pour ¼ cup of the pancake batter in the pan. Cook for 3 minutes per side or until cooked through. Repeat with remaining pancakes.

While the pancakes are cooking, heat the maple syrup in a small saucepan over low heat until just warmed. Remove from the heat and stir in the vanilla extract.

Pour the warm syrup over the pancakes to serve.

BREAKFAST WITH
a twist

♤♡♤♡♤♡♤♡♤♡♤♡♤♡♤♡♤

This chapter is full of fun-filled break-fast options with a bit of a twist! From pancakes masquerading as donuts, to French toast and a breakfast sandwich, this chapter has classic breakfast recipes with the fun amped up.

♤♡♤♡♤♡♤♡♤♡♤♡♤♡♤♡♤

MAPLE-GLAZED BACON PANCAKES

Have you ever tried the maple-glazed donuts dotted with crumbles of bacon from a donut shop? To die for! I'm obsessed with that salty-sweet combo and firmly believe that bacon makes everything better. So, it should come as no surprise that I made Maple-Glazed Bacon Pancakes! They're just as good as the donut version, but don't require deep frying.

Prep Time: 15 minutes
Cook Time: 10 minutes
Total Time: 25 minutes
Yield: 8 (4-inch) pancakes

6 strips bacon
1 cup flour
1 tsp. baking powder
½ tsp. baking soda
½ tsp. ground cinnamon
¼ tsp. salt
1 cup buttermilk
1 egg, beaten
1 Tbsp. maple syrup
1 Tbsp. vegetable oil
1 tsp. vanilla extract
Maple Glaze, page 147

In a large skillet over medium heat, fry the bacon until crisp, turning halfway through. Drain on a paper towel-lined sheet until cool enough to crumble into pieces with your fingers. Set aside ¼ of the bacon crumbles for topping the pancakes. Use the remaining ¾ of the bacon for the pancake batter.

Heat a large skillet or griddle over medium heat.

In a medium bowl, combine the flour, baking powder, baking soda, cinnamon, and salt. Whisk to combine.

In a small bowl, mix together the buttermilk, egg, maple syrup, oil, and vanilla.

Stir the wet ingredients into the dry ingredients until combined but still slightly lumpy.

Stir in the crumbled bacon.

Pour ¼ cup of batter onto a heated griddle or skillet. Cook for 3 minutes or until bubbles have formed on the surface and popped. Flip the pancake and continue cooking until cooked through. Repeat with remaining batter.

Top with Maple Glaze and sprinkle on the reserved bacon crumbles.

MAPLE-GLAZED BACON PANCAKES

HOECAKES

Cornbread has always been a staple in my family. My parents made it a few times a week when we were growing up, and I always serve it with chili. These hoecakes aren't like that traditional corn bread I grew up eating, but these little cakes are what I usually make these days. They work perfectly alongside a bowl of chili, but my favorite way to eat them is topped with butter and doused in honey.

Prep Time: 5 minutes
Cook Time: 10 minutes
Total Time: 15 minutes
Yield: 12 (2-inch) pancakes

¼ cup butter, for frying
½ cup flour
½ cup cornmeal
1 Tbsp. sugar
1 tsp. baking powder
½ tsp. baking soda
¼ tsp. salt
¾ cup buttermilk
1 egg, beaten
1 Tbsp. oil

Heat a large skillet over medium heat and add 2 tablespoons of butter to cover the bottom of the pan. Let butter melt while you prepare the pancakes.

In a medium bowl, combine the flour, cornmeal, sugar, baking powder, baking soda, and salt. Whisk to combine.

In a small bowl, mix together the buttermilk, egg, and oil.

Stir the wet ingredients into the dry ingredients until combined but still slightly lumpy.

Pour 2 tablespoons of batter into the hot skillet. Cook for 2 minutes or until bubbles have formed on the surface and popped. Flip the pancake and continue cooking until cooked through. Repeat with remaining batter, adding more butter to the pan as needed.

Serve with honey and butter.

CINNAMON SUGAR DONUT PANCAKES

Ah, yes. Cinnamon sugar donuts. They're my absolute, all-time favorites. I had to make a pancake version, and they do not disappoint. These get dunked in melted butter and then tossed in a cinnamon sugar mixture, giving these pancakes a slightly crunchy exterior with a warm, almost melty interior.

Prep Time: 5 minutes
Cook Time: 10 minutes
Total Time: 15 minutes
Yield: 8 (4-inch) pancakes

For the pancakes:
1 cup flour
2 Tbsp. sugar
1 tsp. cinnamon
1 tsp. baking powder
½ tsp. baking soda
¼ tsp. salt
1 cup buttermilk
1 egg, beaten
2 Tbsp. vegetable oil
1 tsp. vanilla extract

For the topping:
½ cup butter, melted
⅓ cup granulated sugar
¾ tsp. ground cinnamon

Heat a large skillet or griddle over medium heat.

In a medium bowl, combine the flour, sugar, cinnamon, baking powder, baking soda, and salt. Whisk to combine.

In a small bowl, mix together the buttermilk, egg, oil, and vanilla.

Stir the wet ingredients into the dry ingredients until combined but still slightly lumpy.

Pour ¼ cup of batter onto a heated griddle or skillet. Cook for 3 minutes or until bubbles have formed on the surface and popped. Flip the pancake and continue cooking until cooked through. Repeat with remaining batter.

To make the topping, place the melted butter in a large, shallow dish, such as a pie plate. In a second, large, shallow dish, mix together the sugar and cinnamon.

Quickly dunk each pancake into the melted butter, turning to coat each side. Transfer the buttery pancake to the cinnamon sugar mixture and coat each side.

Serve immediately.

BREAKFAST SANDWICHES

We usually go for a biscuit sandwich when it comes to breakfast, but while I was making a batch of pancakes to serve with our sausage and eggs, I decided to throw them all together in a sandwich, and boy, were these good. You can certainly mix these up and use bacon or ham instead of sausage. We like these with runny eggs, but top them with whatever type of egg you like!

Prep Time: 20 minutes
Cook Time: 20 minutes
Total Time: 40 minutes
Yield: 5 sandwiches

For the pancakes:
1 cup flour
2 Tbsp. sugar
1 tsp. cinnamon
1 tsp. baking powder
½ tsp. baking soda
¼ tsp. salt
1 cup buttermilk
1 egg, beaten
2 Tbsp. maple syrup
2 Tbsp. vegetable oil
1 tsp. vanilla extract

For making the sandwiches:
5 eggs
5 sausage patties
5 slices cheddar cheese

Heat a large skillet or griddle over medium heat.

In a medium bowl, combine the flour, sugar, cinnamon, baking powder, baking soda, and salt. Whisk to combine.

In a small bowl, mix together the buttermilk, egg, maple syrup, oil, and vanilla.

Stir the wet ingredients into the dry ingredients until combined but still slightly lumpy.

Pour ¼ cup of batter onto a heated griddle or skillet. Cook for 3 minutes or until bubbles have formed on the surface and popped. Flip the pancake and continue cooking until cooked through. Repeat with remaining batter.

While the pancakes are cooking, heat a nonstick skillet over medium heat, spray with nonstick spray, and crack the egg in the pan. Cook until the whites are opaque and gently flip. Continue cooking until the yolk is as done as you like.

Set eggs aside and add the sausage patties to the skillet. Cook them for 5 minutes per side or until cooked through. Top with a slice of cheese.

To build your sandwiches, place one sausage patty with cheese on top of half of the pancakes. Place the egg on top of the sausage, and then top with the remaining pancakes.

Serve immediately.

FRENCH TOAST PANCAKES

My husband tends to leave the cooking to me, but every year on Mother's Day he serves us all French toast. I never make French toast myself, since it's the one dish he makes, and I almost felt a little guilty making his signature dish into pancakes. Then we all took a bite, and that guilt flew right out the window! This breakfast really is the best of both worlds . . . pancakes and French toast all in one!

Prep Time: 10 minutes
Cook Time: 20 minutes
Total Time: 30 minutes
Yield: 8 (4-inch) pancakes

For the pancakes:
1 cup flour
2 Tbsp. sugar
1 tsp. cinnamon
1 tsp. baking powder
½ tsp. baking soda
¼ tsp. salt
1 cup buttermilk
1 egg, beaten
2 Tbsp. vegetable oil
1 tsp. vanilla extract

For making the French toast:
2 eggs
½ cup milk
¼ tsp. ground cinnamon

Heat a large skillet or griddle over medium heat.

In a medium bowl, combine the flour, sugar, cinnamon, baking powder, baking soda, and salt. Whisk to combine.

In a small bowl, mix together the buttermilk, egg, oil, and vanilla.

Stir the wet ingredients into the dry ingredients until combined but still slightly lumpy.

Pour ¼ cup of batter onto a heated griddle or skillet. Cook for 3 minutes or until bubbles have formed on the surface and popped. Flip the pancake and continue cooking until cooked through. Repeat with remaining batter.

Set pancakes aside until cool enough to handle. Meanwhile, in a shallow dish, such as a pie plate, whisk together the eggs, milk, and cinnamon.

Dip each pancake in the egg mixture and let sit for 15 seconds per side. Transfer to the griddle and cook for 2 more minutes per side.

Serve with maple syrup, whipped cream, and fresh fruit, as desired.

PEANUT BUTTER & JELLY PANCAKES

I don't know a child that doesn't love a peanut butter and jelly sandwich for lunch! It's a favorite, for sure. My kids love when I bring this classic sandwich to the breakfast table with these PB&J pancakes. The pancakes get a little boost of protein from the peanut butter, and that helps keep their bellies full too.

Prep Time: 5 minutes
Cook Time: 10 minutes
Total Time: 15 minutes
Yield: 8 (4-inch) pancakes

1 cup flour
2 Tbsp. sugar
1 tsp. baking powder
½ tsp. baking soda
¼ tsp. salt
1 cup buttermilk
1 egg, beaten
⅓ cup creamy peanut butter
Strawberry Syrup, page 139

Heat a large skillet or griddle over medium heat.

In a medium bowl, combine the flour, sugar, baking powder, baking soda, and salt. Whisk to combine.

In a small bowl, mix together the buttermilk, egg, and peanut butter.

Stir the wet ingredients into the dry ingredients until combined but still slightly lumpy.

Spray your cooking surface with nonstick cooking spray, and place ¼ cup of the pancake batter in the pan. The batter is very thick and will need to be spread a bit with the back of a spoon, spatula, or your ¼-cup measure. Cook for 3 minutes per side or until cooked through. Repeat with remaining pancakes.

Pour on Strawberry Syrup before serving.

breakfast with a twist

GLAZED DONUT PANCAKES

I'm a bit of a donut lover (and that's putting it mildly!), so I knew that I couldn't write a cookbook without incorporating a donut recipe or two! These glazed donut pancakes are a perfect marriage of two breakfast favorites, without the hassle of frying.

Prep Time: 10 minutes
Time: 10 minutes
Total Time: 20 minutes
Yield: 8 (4-inch) pancake donuts and holes

For the pancakes:

1 cup flour
1 Tbsp. sugar
1 tsp. ground cinnamon
1 tsp. baking powder
½ tsp. baking soda
¼ tsp. salt
1 cup buttermilk
1 egg, beaten
2 Tbsp. vegetable oil
1 tsp. vanilla extract

For the glaze:

2 cups powdered sugar
3½ Tbsp. milk
1 tsp. vanilla extract
sprinkles, if desired

Heat a large skillet or griddle over medium heat.

In a medium bowl, combine the flour, sugar, cinnamon, baking powder, baking soda, and salt. Whisk to combine.

In a small bowl, mix together the buttermilk, egg, oil, and vanilla.

Stir the wet ingredients into the dry ingredients until combined but still slightly lumpy.

Pour a scant ¼ cup of batter (about 3 tablespoons) onto a heated griddle or skillet. Cook for 3 minutes or until bubbles have formed on the surface and have popped. Flip the pancake and continue cooking until cooked through. Repeat with remaining batter.

When donuts are cool enough to handle, use a small donut cutter to cut the centers out of the donuts. The cap from a 20-ounce water or soda bottle works great for cutting centers too.

To make the glaze, bring a small pot of 2 inches of water to a simmer over medium heat. Add the powdered sugar, milk, and vanilla to a large glass bowl. Whisk together and place the bowl over the pot of water. Remove the pan from the heat, but keep the glaze over the water to keep it warm and runny.

Carefully dip the donuts into the glaze using your fingers or a fork. The bottom of the bowl will be hot.

Transfer the glazed donuts to a wire rack with a sheet of parchment under it to catch drips. Sprinkle immediately with sprinkles, if desired. Let the donut pancakes sit for 5 minutes before serving.

HONEY BUN PANCAKES

These sweet pancakes have a double dose of honey—making them extra special. The honey swirl really sets these apart from other pancakes, and when they're topped with buttermilk syrup, your whole family will gobble them right up.

Prep Time: 5 minutes
Cook Time: 10 minutes
Total Time: 15 minutes
Yield: 8 (4-inch) pancakes

1 cup flour
1½ tsp. ground cinnamon, divided
1 tsp. baking powder
½ tsp. baking soda
¼ tsp. salt
1 cup buttermilk
1 egg, beaten
2 Tbsp. vegetable oil
6 Tbsp. honey, divided
1 tsp. vanilla extract
Buttermilk syrup, page 155

Heat a large skillet or griddle over medium heat.

In a medium bowl, combine the flour, baking powder, baking soda, ¾ teaspoon ground cinnamon, and salt. Whisk to combine.

In a small bowl, mix together the buttermilk, egg, oil, 2 tablespoons of honey, and vanilla.

Stir the wet ingredients into the dry ingredients until combined but still slightly lumpy.

Combine the remaining 4 tablespoons of honey and the remaining ¾ teaspoon of cinnamon together and stir until well combined. Add to a squeeze bottle.

Pour ¼ cup of batter onto a heated griddle or skillet. Start at the center of your pancake and squeeze the honey mixture in a swirl, much like a cinnamon roll. Cook for 3 minutes or until bubbles have formed on the surface and popped. Flip the pancake and continue cooking until cooked through. Repeat with remaining batter.

Top with Buttermilk Syrup.

BROWN SUGAR PANCAKES
WITH CINNAMON STREUSEL

I'm a self-proclaimed streusel addict! I could (and sometimes do!) eat the mixture with a spoon. It's simple to make with just a few everyday ingredients, and it really takes these pancakes to another level. They don't need syrup, but of course adding some wouldn't hurt anything either.

Prep Time: 10 minutes
Cook Time: 10 minutes
Total Time: 20 minutes
Yield: 8 (4-inch) pancakes

For the cinnamon streusel:
3 Tbsp. brown sugar
2 Tbsp. flour
2 Tbsp. rolled oats
2 Tbsp. cold butter
½ tsp. ground cinnamon

For the pancakes:
1 cup flour
2 Tbsp. brown sugar
1 tsp. baking powder
½ tsp. baking soda
½ tsp. ground cinnamon
¼ tsp. salt
1 cup buttermilk
1 egg, beaten
2 Tbsp. vegetable oil
1 tsp. vanilla extract

To begin, prepare the streusel. Add brown sugar, flour, oats, butter, and cinnamon to a small bowl and combine with a pastry cutter until your mixture resembles coarse crumbs.

To make the pancakes, heat a large skillet or griddle over medium heat.

In a medium bowl, combine the flour, brown sugar, baking powder, baking soda, cinnamon, and salt. Whisk to combine.

In a small bowl, mix together the buttermilk, egg, oil, and vanilla.

Stir the wet ingredients into the dry ingredients until combined but still slightly lumpy.

Pour ¼ cup of batter onto a heated griddle or skillet. Cook for 3 minutes or until bubbles have formed on the surface and popped. Sprinkle 1 tablespoon of streusel over the top of the pancake. Carefully flip the pancake and continue cooking until cooked through. Repeat with remaining batter.

CINNAMON ROLL PANCAKES

If I had to choose one recipe out of this book that I'm most excited about, it'd probably be this one. I mean, look at these perfect little pancake rolls! So adorable and easier to make than you'd think! My kids adore cinnamon rolls, and they enthusiastically gobble these little rolls up anytime I make them.

Prep Time: 5 minutes
Cook Time: 10 minutes
Total Time: 15 minutes
Yield: 24 mini rolls

For the pancakes:
1 cup flour
2 Tbsp. sugar
1 tsp. baking powder
½ tsp. baking soda
¼ tsp. salt
1 cup buttermilk
1 egg, beaten
2 Tbsp. vegetable oil
1 tsp. vanilla extract

For the filling:
¼ cup butter, melted
½ cup brown sugar
1 tsp. ground cinnamon

For the glaze:
1 cup powdered sugar
1 Tbsp. milk

Heat a large skillet or griddle over medium heat.

In a medium bowl, combine the flour, sugar, baking powder, baking soda, and salt. Whisk to combine.

In a small bowl, mix together the buttermilk, egg, oil, and vanilla.

Stir the wet ingredients into the dry ingredients until combined but still slightly lumpy.

Spray your cooking surface with nonstick cooking spray, and place ½ cup of the pancake batter in the pan in an oblong shape. Cook for 3 minutes per side or until cooked through. Repeat with remaining batter to make 3 large oblong pancakes.

While the pancakes are cooking, stir together the melted butter, brown sugar, and cinnamon to make the filling. Lay the pancakes out flat and spread ⅓ of the filling over each pancake.

Starting with the short end, roll the pancakes as tightly as possible without breaking them, like a cinnamon roll. Place 4 toothpicks in each pancake to hold them together. Use a sharp knife to cut between each toothpick to make 24 miniature rolls.

To make the glaze, whisk together the powdered sugar and milk until smooth. Drizzle over the rolls.

HEALTHIER
pancakes

It was important to me to include some healthier options in this book, but it was just as important that I not sacrifice flavor to do so. I used more nutritious flours, loaded them up with protein where I could, and snuck in as many vitamins as possible. My family devoured every pancake in this chapter without a bit of complaint.

MATCHA PANCAKES

Matcha powder is just ground green tea leaves, but it packs a powerful punch! You get to enjoy all of the vitamins and minerals loaded in the tea leaves. I've snuck some matcha in these pancakes, giving them a delightful green color, nutrients, vitamins, antioxidants, and amino acids. Matcha can be bitter, so I've just used 2 teaspoons of it, but you can certainly increase that up to 2 tablespoons for a more powerful flavor and a boost of nutrition.

Prep Time: 5 minutes
Cook Time: 10 minutes
Yield: 8 4-inch pancakes

½ cup whole wheat flour
½ cup white flour
2 tsp. matcha powder
1 tsp. baking powder
½ tsp. baking soda
¼ tsp. salt
1 cup buttermilk
2 Tbsp. maple syrup
1 egg, beaten
1 tsp. vanilla extract

Heat a large skillet or griddle over medium heat.

In a medium bowl, combine the flours, matcha powder, baking powder, baking soda, and salt. Whisk to combine.

In a small bowl, mix together the buttermilk, syrup, egg, and vanilla.

Stir the wet ingredients into the dry ingredients until combined but still slightly lumpy.

Spray your cooking surface with nonstick cooking spray and place ¼ cup of the pancake batter in the pan. Cook for 3 minutes per side or until cooked through. Repeat with remaining pancakes.

APPLESAUCE PANCAKES

These pancakes are packed full of applesauce, making them perfect for any apple lover. The whole kitchen will smell like fall while these are cooking too. The applesauce makes these extra moist, but they stay nice and puffy! I used cinnamon applesauce here, but plain works great as well. If you use unsweetened applesauce, you might consider adding a tablespoon of sugar or honey to the batter.

Prep Time: 5 minutes
Cook Time: 10 minutes
Yield: 6 (4-inch) pancakes

½ cup whole wheat flour
½ cup white flour
1 tsp. baking powder
1 tsp. cinnamon
½ tsp. baking soda
¼ tsp. salt
1 cup applesauce
1 egg, beaten
2 Tbsp. buttermilk
1 tsp. vanilla extract

Heat a large skillet or griddle over medium heat.

In a medium bowl, combine the flour, baking powder, cinnamon, baking soda, and salt. Whisk to combine.

In a small bowl, mix together the applesauce, egg, buttermilk, and vanilla.

Stir the wet ingredients into the dry ingredients until combined but still slightly lumpy.

Spray your cooking surface with nonstick cooking spray and place ¼ cup of the pancake batter in the pan. Cook for 3 minutes per side or until cooked through. Repeat with remaining pancakes.

BLUEBERRY ALMOND BUTTER PANCAKES

Two foods that seem to always be lurking around my house are blueberries and almond butter, so I knew that I needed to find a way to combine them. These pancakes are fantastically creamy, and the little pops of berries really complete them. Serve them with maple syrup or an extra smear of almond butter.

Prep Time: 5 minutes
Cook Time: 10 minutes
Total Time: 15 minutes
Yield: 8 (4-inch) pancakes

½ cup whole wheat flour
½ cup white flour
2 Tbsp. brown sugar
1 tsp. baking powder
½ tsp. baking soda
¼ tsp. ground cinnamon
¼ tsp. salt
⅓ cup almond butter
1 cup buttermilk
1 egg, beaten
1 tsp. vanilla extract
½ cup blueberries, rinsed and dried
Blueberry Maple Syrup, page 159

Heat a large skillet or griddle over medium heat.

In a medium bowl, combine the whole wheat flour, white flour, sugar, baking powder, baking soda, salt, and cinnamon. Whisk to combine.

In a small bowl, microwave the almond butter for 20 seconds or until smooth and somewhat melted.

In a small bowl, mix together the buttermilk, egg, almond butter, and vanilla.

Stir the wet ingredients into the dry ingredients until combined but still slightly lumpy.

Spray your cooking surface with nonstick cooking spray and place ¼ cup of the pancake batter in the pan. The batter will be quite thick. Use the back of a spoon or the bottom of your measuring cup to gently spread the batter into a 4-inch circle. Press 4 or 5 blueberries into each pancake. Cook for 3 minutes per side or until cooked through. Repeat with remaining pancakes.

Top with Blueberry Maple Syrup from page 159 or extra almond butter.

APPLE CINNAMON OATMEAL PANCAKES

My kids adore those little packets of instant oatmeal, and they always go straight for the apple cinnamon flavor. These pancakes are loaded with oats, applesauce, and cinnamon for a fresh new take on that bowl of oatmeal. The applesauce keeps these extra moist without adding any extra fat, and the whole grains are sure to help keep little tummies full. We serve these with extra applesauce on top, but maple syrup would be great too.

Prep Time: 5 minutes
Cook Time: 10 minutes
Total Time: 15 minutes
Yield: 8 (4-inch) pancakes

½ cup rolled oats or oat flour
½ cup whole wheat flour
1 tsp. ground cinnamon
1 tsp. baking powder
½ tsp. baking soda
¼ tsp. salt
1 cup applesauce
1 egg, beaten
2 Tbsp. buttermilk
1 tsp. vanilla extract

To make your own oat flour, add ½ cup of rolled oats to a blender or food processor and process until you have a fine powder.

Heat a large skillet or griddle over medium heat.

In a medium bowl, combine the oat flour, wheat flour, cinnamon, baking powder, baking soda, and salt. Whisk to combine.

In a small bowl, mix together the applesauce, egg, buttermilk, and vanilla.

Stir the wet ingredients into the dry ingredients until combined but still slightly lumpy.

Spray your cooking surface with nonstick cooking spray and place ¼ cup of the pancake batter in the pan. The batter will be quite thick. Use the back of a spoon or the bottom of your measuring cup to gently spread the batter into a 4-inch circle. Cook for 3 minutes per side or until cooked through. Repeat with remaining pancakes.

Top with extra applesauce or syrup, as desired.

CINNAMON RAISIN BREAD PANCAKES

I can't even smell these pancakes without thinking of my grandma! She has a slice of cinnamon raisin bread, toasted and smeared with butter, for breakfast every morning. I just know she would love these pancakes! They're loaded with raisins and have a hearty texture from the whole wheat flour. The cinnamon syrup is just the icing on the cake.

Prep Time: 10 minutes
Cook Time: 10 minutes
Total Time: 20 minutes
Yield: 8 (4-inch) pancakes

¾ cup raisins
1 cup whole wheat flour
2 Tbsp. brown sugar
1 tsp. baking powder
½ tsp. baking soda
¼ tsp. salt
1 cup buttermilk
1 egg, beaten
2 Tbsp. melted butter
1 tsp. vanilla extract
Cinnamon Syrup, for serving, from page 151

Add the raisins and ½ cup of water to a small sauce pan. Turn on the heat to medium and bring to a boil. Remove from the heat and drain the water. Set raisins aside.

Heat a large skillet or griddle over medium heat.

In a medium bowl, combine the flour, sugar, baking powder, baking soda, and salt. Whisk to combine. Stir in the raisins.

In a small bowl, mix together the buttermilk, egg, butter, and vanilla.

Stir the wet ingredients into the dry ingredients until combined but still slightly lumpy.

Spray your cooking surface with nonstick cooking spray and place ¼ cup of the pancake batter in the pan. Cook for 3 minutes per side or until cooked through. Repeat with remaining pancakes.

Serve with Cinnamon Syrup from page 151.

WHOLE WHEAT FLAXSEED PANCAKES

My kids eat plenty of white flour products. After all, my blog is full of completely unhealthy baked goods. The thing is, when it comes to pancakes, they are just as happy to eat a stack of these whole wheat flaxseed cakes as they are the more traditional buttermilk version made with white flour. That's because these pancakes are just as moist and fluffy as their counterpart. The flax gives them a nice little boost of vitamins and fiber.

Prep Time: 5 minutes
Cook Time: 10 minutes
Total Time: 15 minutes
Yield: 8 (4-inch) pancakes

1 cup whole wheat flour
¼ cup flaxseed
1 Tbsp. brown sugar
1 tsp. baking powder
½ tsp. baking soda
½ tsp. ground cinnamon
¼ tsp. salt
1¼ cups buttermilk
1 egg, beaten
1 Tbsp. butter, melted
1 tsp. vanilla extract

Heat a large skillet or griddle over medium heat.

In a medium bowl, combine the flour, flaxseed, sugar, baking powder, baking soda, cinnamon, and salt. Whisk to combine.

In a small bowl, mix together the buttermilk, egg, butter, and vanilla.

Stir the wet ingredients into the dry ingredients until combined but still slightly lumpy.

Spray your cooking surface with nonstick cooking spray and place ¼ cup of the pancake batter in the pan. Cook for 3 minutes per side or until cooked through. Repeat with remaining pancakes.

WHOLE WHEAT BUTTERNUT SQUASH PANCAKES

Sneaking foods my kids don't like into their pancakes has become a bit of a hobby of mine. Luckily for them, butternut squash takes on an entirely new flavor when it's paired with a bit of cinnamon and cooked into a pancake! You can certainly purée your own squash, but I've found that using a jar of baby food works just as well.

Prep Time: 10 minutes
Cook Time: 10 minutes
Total Time: 20 minutes
Yield: 8 (4-inch) pancakes

½ cup whole wheat flour
½ cup white flour
2 Tbsp. brown sugar
1 tsp. ground cinnamon
1 tsp. baking powder
½ tsp. baking soda
½ tsp. salt
¼ tsp. nutmeg
¾ cup buttermilk
¼ cup butternut squash purée
1 egg, beaten
1 Tbsp. vegetable oil
1 tsp. vanilla extract

Heat a large skillet or griddle over medium heat.

In a medium bowl, combine both flours, sugar, cinnamon, baking powder, baking soda, salt, and nutmeg. Whisk to combine.

In a small bowl, mix together the buttermilk, squash, egg, oil, and vanilla.

Stir the wet ingredients into the dry ingredients until combined but still slightly lumpy.

Spray your cooking surface with nonstick cooking spray and place ¼ cup of the pancake batter in the pan. Cook for 3 minutes per side or until cooked through. Repeat with remaining pancakes.

WHOLE WHEAT SWEET POTATO OATMEAL PANCAKES

Sweet potatoes are an all-time favorite around here. I like to keep cans of sweet potatoes or yams in the pantry to make my own purée, but you can roast a whole sweet potato in the oven and purée that if you'd prefer. You can also swap in pumpkin purée for the sweet potato. The flavor of the sweet potato combined with the texture of the whole wheat flour and oats makes these pancakes special. To me, they taste like fall.

Prep Time: 10 minutes
Cook Time: 10 minutes
Total Time: 20 minutes
Yield: 8 (4-inch) pancakes

½ cup whole wheat flour
½ cup rolled oats or oat flour
2 Tbsp. brown sugar
1 tsp. ground cinnamon
1 tsp. baking powder
½ tsp. baking soda
½ tsp. salt
¼ tsp. nutmeg
1 cup buttermilk
1 egg, beaten
2 Tbsp. vegetable oil
1 tsp. vanilla extract
½ cup sweet potato purée

To make your own oat flour, add ½ cup of rolled oats to a blender or food processor and process until you have a fine powder.

Heat a large skillet or griddle over medium heat.

In a medium bowl, combine the flour, oat flour, sugar, cinnamon, baking powder, baking soda, salt, and nutmeg. Whisk to combine.

In a small bowl, mix together the buttermilk, egg, oil, vanilla, and sweet potato purée.

Stir the wet ingredients into the dry ingredients until combined but still slightly lumpy.

Spray your cooking surface with nonstick cooking spray and place ¼ cup of the pancake batter in the pan. Cook for 3 minutes per side or until cooked through. Repeat with remaining pancakes.

STRAWBERRY RICOTTA WHOLE WHEAT PANCAKES

These pancakes are packed with protein from the creamy ricotta cheese mixed in the batter. That creaminess stays with the pancakes all through cooking, leaving the centers moist and luscious. Top with fresh strawberries and homemade strawberry syrup and you have one decadent breakfast that almost melts in your mouth.

Prep Time: 5 minutes
Cook Time: 10 minutes
Total Time: 15 minutes
Yield: 10 (4-inch) pancakes

1 cup whole wheat flour
1 Tbsp. brown sugar
1 tsp. baking powder
½ tsp. baking soda
¼ tsp. salt
1 cup buttermilk
¾ cup part-skim ricotta cheese
1 egg, beaten
1 Tbsp. vegetable oil
1 tsp. vanilla extract
½ cup chopped strawberries, for serving
Strawberry Syrup, for serving, on page 139

Heat a large skillet or griddle over medium heat.

In a medium bowl, combine the flour, sugar, baking powder, baking soda, and salt. Whisk to combine.

In a small bowl, mix together the buttermilk, ricotta, egg, oil, and vanilla.

Stir the wet ingredients into the dry ingredients until combined but still slightly lumpy.

Spray your cooking surface with nonstick cooking spray and place ¼ cup of the pancake batter in the pan. Cook for 3 minutes per side or until cooked through. Repeat with remaining pancakes.

Serve with chopped strawberries and strawberry syrup from page 139.

STRAWBERRY RICOTTA WHOLE WHEAT PANCAKES

LEMON FLAXSEED PANCAKES

Flaxseed is full of nutrients, vitamins, and fiber, making it a breakfast powerhouse. I paired it with lemon for a bright, fresh flavor in these pancakes.

Prep Time: 5 minutes
Cook Time: 10 minutes
Total Time: 15 minutes
Yield: 8 (4-inch) pancakes

---

1 cup whole wheat flour
¼ cup ground flaxseed
1 Tbsp. brown sugar
1 tsp. baking powder
½ tsp. baking soda
¼ tsp. salt
Zest of 1 lemon
1 cup milk
2 Tbsp. lemon juice
1 egg, beaten
1 Tbsp. vegetable oil
1 tsp. vanilla extract

Heat a large skillet or griddle over medium heat.

In a medium bowl, combine the flour, flaxseed, sugar, baking powder, baking soda, salt, and lemon zest. Whisk to combine.

In a small bowl, mix together the milk, lemon juice, egg, oil, and vanilla.

Stir the wet ingredients into the dry ingredients until combined.

Spray your cooking surface with nonstick cooking spray and place ¼ cup of the pancake batter in the pan. Cook for 3 minutes per side or until cooked through. Repeat with remaining pancakes.

healthier pancakes

73

BLUEBERRY COCONUT QUINOA PANCAKES

These pancakes are packed with both flavor and nutrients. You'll have quinoa left over, and it makes an excellent side dish or breakfast on its own, but you can also keep it in the fridge for a couple of days or freeze it for the next time you plan to make these pancakes.

Prep Time: 5 minutes
Cook Time: 35 minutes
Total Time: 40 minutes
Yield: 8 (4-inch) pancakes

½ cup quinoa
1 cup unsweetened coconut milk
½ cup whole wheat flour
2 Tbsp. brown sugar
1 tsp. baking powder
½ tsp. baking soda
¼ tsp. salt
¾ cup buttermilk
1 egg, beaten
2 Tbsp. melted coconut oil
1 tsp. vanilla
½ cup blueberries

Rinse the quinoa well in cold water. Place in a small saucepan with the coconut milk and bring to a boil over medium-high heat. Once boiling, reduce heat to low, cover, and continue cooking for 20 minutes or until the liquid has evaporated. Remove from heat and let sit for 10 minutes. Fluff with a fork to create 1 cup quinoa.

Heat a large skillet or griddle over medium heat.

In a medium bowl, combine 1 cup of the prepared quinoa, flour, sugar, baking powder, baking soda, and salt. Whisk to combine.

In a small bowl, mix together the buttermilk, egg, coconut oil, and vanilla.

Stir the wet ingredients into the dry ingredients until combined but still slightly lumpy.

Spray your cooking surface with nonstick cooking spray and place ¼ cup of the pancake batter in the pan. Place 4–5 berries on each pancake. Use your finger or a spoon to gently spread a bit of batter over each berry. Cook for 3 minutes per side or until cooked through. Repeat with remaining pancakes.

PUMPKIN QUINOA CAKES

These scrumptious little pancakes are moist and full of pumpkin flavor. The texture of the quinoa is present, but not overwhelming, meaning that even my picky kids will eat these right up. We love them with a sweet browned butter drizzle, but a bit of maple syrup is nice too.

Prep Time: 5 minutes
Cook Time: 35 minutes
Total Time: 40 minutes
Yield: 8 (4-inch) pancakes

½ cup quinoa
1 cup water
¾ cup whole wheat flour
2 Tbsp. brown sugar
1 tsp. ground cinnamon
1 tsp. baking powder
½ tsp. baking soda
¼ tsp. salt
¾ cup pumpkin purée
½ cup buttermilk
1 egg, beaten
1 tsp. vanilla
Browned Butter Drizzle, for serving,
  on page 140

Rinse the quinoa well in cold water. Place in a small saucepan with water and bring to a boil over medium-high heat. Once boiling, reduce heat to low, cover, and continue cooking for 20 minutes or until the liquid has evaporated. Remove from the heat and let sit for 10 minutes. Fluff with a fork.

Heat a large skillet or griddle over medium heat.

In a medium bowl, combine 1 cup of the prepared quinoa, flour, sugar, cinnamon, baking powder, baking soda, and salt. Whisk to combine.

In a small bowl, mix together the pumpkin, buttermilk, egg, and vanilla.

Stir the wet ingredients into the dry ingredients until combined but still slightly lumpy.

Spray your cooking surface with nonstick cooking spray and place ¼ cup of the pancake batter in the pan. Cook for 3 minutes per side or until cooked through. Repeat with remaining pancakes.

Serve with browned butter drizzle, page 140, or maple syrup.

Tip: This recipe will produce close to 2 cups of quinoa, but the leftovers are perfect for a quick side dish. You can also freeze this or store it in the fridge for a couple of days for the next time you make these pancakes.

BLUEBERRY GREEK YOGURT PANCAKES

These pancakes are packed with fresh blueberries and loaded with protein from the addition of Greek yogurt. I also swapped out the white sugar for a bit of raw honey. I would happily eat these for breakfast every day of the week. You can stir the berries right into the batter, but I find that turns them a funky shade of blue, so I prefer to pop them on top of each pancake after pouring the batter in the pan.

Prep Time: 5 minutes
Cook Time: 10 minutes
Total Time: 15 minutes
Yield: 6 (4-inch) pancakes

1 cup whole wheat flour
1 tsp. sugar
1 tsp. baking powder
½ tsp. baking soda
½ tsp. salt
¾ cup buttermilk
⅓ cup fat-free Greek yogurt
1 egg, beaten
1 tsp. vanilla extract
¾ cup blueberries

Heat a large skillet or griddle over medium heat.

In a medium bowl, combine the flour, sugar, baking powder, baking soda, and salt. Whisk to combine.

In a small bowl, mix together the buttermilk, yogurt, egg, and vanilla.

Stir the wet ingredients into the dry ingredients until combined but still slightly lumpy.

Spray your cooking surface with nonstick cooking spray and place ¼ cup of the pancake batter in the pan. Place 4–5 berries on each pancake. Use your finger or a spoon to gently spread a bit of batter over each berry. Cook for 3 minutes per side or until cooked through. Repeat with remaining pancakes.

SAVORY
pancakes

♤♡♤♡♤♡♤♡♤♡♤♡♤♡♤

Sneaking pancakes onto the dinner table is a surefire way to get kids excited to clear their plates! Some of the recipes in this chapter make excellent side dishes, others work well as appetizers, and still others make fantastic main dishes.

♤♡♤♡♤♡♤♡♤♡♤♡♤♡♤

OVEN-FRIED CHICKEN AND PANCAKES

If you're not a Southerner, I may have just lost you with this recipe. I beg you to stick through this one though. Chicken and waffles is a Southern staple, and I've just mixed things up a bit with pancakes. Even if you can't imagine dipping your chicken in maple syrup (but you really should give it a try . . . pure heaven!), this is my all-time favorite way to make my kids chicken nuggets. They're fried in butter right in the oven, and they take almost no time at all to throw together. Serve them with miniature pancakes and plenty of syrup for a fun Southern treat!

Prep Time: 20 minutes
Cook Time: 20 minutes
Total Time: 40 minutes
Yield: 4 servings

For the chicken nuggets:

1 lb. boneless, skinless chicken breasts
2 cups panko breadcrumbs
1 cup flour
1 egg
1 Tbsp. milk
1 Tbsp. hot pepper sauce
1 tsp. salt
1 tsp. pepper
8 Tbsp. butter

For the pancakes:

1 cup flour
1 tsp. baking powder
½ tsp. baking soda
½ tsp. ground cinnamon
¼ tsp. salt
1 cup buttermilk
1 egg, beaten
1 Tbsp. maple syrup
1 Tbsp. vegetable oil
1 tsp. vanilla extract
Bacon (optional)

To make the chicken nuggets, cut chicken into 1-inch chunks.

Get out three shallow dishes, such as pie plates. Add the panko to one dish, the flour to another, and the egg, milk, and hot sauce to a third dish. Whisk together the egg mixture. Sprinkle the salt and pepper into the dish with the flour and stir.

Heat an oven to 375 degrees. Melt the butter and pour it directly onto a rimmed cookie sheet.

Dip the chicken chunks into the flour, then the egg mixture, then the panko. Place the coated chicken on the baking dish in the melted butter.

Bake for 6 minutes, flip, and then continue baking for 8 more minutes.

While the chicken is baking, make the pancakes.

Heat a large skillet or griddle over medium heat.

In a medium bowl, combine the flour, baking powder, baking soda, cinnamon, and salt. Whisk to combine.

In a small bowl, mix together the buttermilk, egg, maple syrup, oil, and vanilla.

Stir the wet ingredients into the dry ingredients until combined but still slightly lumpy.

Optionally, stir in crumbled bacon.

Pour a heaping tablespoon of batter onto a heated griddle or skillet. Cook for 2 minutes, or until bubbles have formed on the surface and have popped. Flip the pancake and continue cooking until cooked through. Repeat with remaining batter.

Serve with maple syrup for dipping.

GARLIC PARMESAN ZUCCHINI CAKES

Zucchini cakes are a perfect way to use up all of that summer zucchini. The outside of these cakes is crispy, and the inside is perfectly moist. These make a great side dish to just about any type of grilled meat.

Prep Time: 10 minutes
Cook Time: 10 minutes
Total Time: 20 minutes
Yield: 10 (2-inch) pancakes

2 medium zucchini
¼ cup flour
1 egg, beaten
2 Tbsp. grated Parmesan
2 cloves garlic, finely grated
½ tsp. salt
Oil, for frying

Wash and grate the zucchini. Add the zucchini, flour, egg, Parmesan, garlic, and salt to a medium bowl and stir to combine.

Heat a large skillet over medium heat and add just enough oil to lightly coat the bottom of the pan.

Drop spoonfuls of the zucchini mixture into the hot oil and flatten lightly with the back of the spoon, leaving at least 1 inch of space between each zucchini cake. Cook for 3 minutes or until the bottoms are golden brown. Flip and continue cooking until browned.

Drain on a paper towel–lined plate and serve warm.

BLT POTATO PANCAKES

I'm a firm believer that bacon makes everything better and that a classic BLT can't be beat. I turned that classic into an appetizer by swapping out the bread for pancakes, fancying up the traditional iceberg lettuce with arugula, and drizzling on a thin garlic mayonnaise. These would make a great lunch and you could easily add extra arugula, bacon, and tomatoes to make it a bit more filling.

Prep Time: 10 minutes

Cook time: 30 minutes

Total Time: 40 minutes

Yield: 6 large-sized appetizers or 12 smaller appetizers

For the pancakes:
2 cups cold mashed potatoes

2 cup flour, plus more as needed

2 eggs, beaten

1 Tbsp. chopped chives

2 tsp. salt

1 tsp. pepper

For the topping:
6 slices bacon

½–1 cup baby arugula, rinsed and dried

½ cup diced tomato

2 Tbsp. mayonnaise

4 tsp. buttermilk

1 tsp. garlic powder

In a medium bowl, combine the potatoes, flour, eggs, chives, salt, and pepper. If you're using leftover mashed potatoes that have already been salted, you may need to reduce the amount of salt you add here. Stir with a fork to combine. The mixture will be thick. Place in the refrigerator while you cook the bacon.

Heat a large skillet over medium heat. Cut each piece of bacon in half and fry until crisp. Drain on a paper towel–lined plate. Do not remove the pan from the heat or drain the grease.

Remove the potatoes from the refrigerator and use your hands to scoop out golf ball–sized amounts of dough. Pat gently into a patty. If the mixture is too sticky, add a bit more flour. The amount of flour needed will vary based on your potatoes. If you're using leftover potatoes that have been mashed with milk and butter, you'll need more flour. If you're using plain mashed potatoes, you'll likely need less flour. Just add flour until the dough is workable.

Carefully place the potato patties into the pan with the bacon grease. Fry until golden brown, about 3 minutes per side. Remove to a paper towel–lined plate to drain.

To make larger appetizers, place two potato pancakes on each plate. Top with a bit of arugula, two slices of bacon, and some diced tomatoes. If you're making smaller appetizers, use one potato cake per plate.

To make the sauce, mix together the mayonnaise, buttermilk, and garlic powder until well combined. Lightly drizzle over the tops.

Serve immediately.

TEX-MEX QUINOA CAKES

Tex-Mex is my favorite type of food, so it goes without saying that I had to incorporate those flavors into this book! I used quinoa as the base for these little cakes; the outside fries up nice and crisp while the inside is soft and full of flavor.

Prep Time: 15 minutes
Cook Time: 40 minutes
Total Time: 55 minutes
Yield: 12 (2-inch) patties

½ cup dry quinoa, rinsed well
1 cup water
1 tsp. chili powder
½ tsp. ground cumin
¼ tsp. garlic powder
¼ tsp. salt
½ cup canned black beans
¼ cup canned or frozen corn
2 Tbsp. chopped cilantro
1 Tbsp. chopped green onions
1 tsp. lime juice
2 eggs
¾–1 cup panko bread crumbs
2 Tbsp. vegetable oil, plus more as needed

Add quinoa, water, chili powder, cumin, garlic powder, and salt to a small sauce pan. Bring to a boil over medium heat, cover, and continue cooking for 20 minutes or until the water has been absorbed. Remove from the heat, stir with a fork, and let sit, covered, for 10 more minutes.

Place the quinoa in a medium bowl and let sit 30 minutes.

Add the beans, corn, cilantro, green onions, lime juice, eggs, and ¾ cup panko to the quinoa and stir to combine. Let sit 5 minutes. Use your hands to scoop up a golf ball–sized amount of quinoa and form into a patty. If the mixture is too wet, add more panko. If the mixture is too dry, add a bit of water, one teaspoon at a time, until the mixture is easily formed into patties.

Heat a large skillet over medium-high heat. Add enough oil to lightly cover the bottom of the pan. When the oil is hot, add the patties to the pan, leaving at least 1-inch space between them. Cook for 3 minutes per side, or until golden brown.

Drain on a paper towel–lined plate.

GARLIC & DILL CAULIFLOWER CAKES

I've always loved the mellow flavor of cauliflower, but my kids just won't go for it. I've finally convinced them to love it by serving up these little cakes with dinner. The garlic and dill add a great flavor, and the cauliflower is nice and smooth, much like a good mashed potato.

Prep Time: 10 minutes
Cook Time: 25 minutes
Total Time: 35 minutes
Yield: 12 (3-inch) cakes

1 head cauliflower
1 clove garlic
2 tsp. dill
1 tsp. salt
½ tsp. black pepper
1 Tbsp. butter
2 eggs, beaten
½ cup flour
2 Tbsp. vegetable oil
Sour cream, for serving

Chop the cauliflower into small florets and rinse. Steam, boil, or microwave the cauliflower until very tender.

Drain the cauliflower and place in a large bowl. Grate the garlic over the cauliflower. Add the dill, salt, pepper, and butter to the bowl. Mash the cauliflower with a potato masher until it is the texture of rice.

Stir the eggs and flour into the cauliflower and mix until just combined.

Heat a medium skillet over medium heat. Add 2 tablespoons of oil to cover the bottom of the pan. Heat to 375 degrees.

When the oil is hot, use a medium-sized cookie scoop (about 1¾ tablespoons) to drop the cauliflower batter gently into the pan of oil. Lightly press the batter down with the back of the scoop. Add as many scoops of batter to the pan as you can without crowding the pan.

Cook for 3 minutes or until the edges are golden brown. Gently use a spatula to flip the cakes over and continue cooking for 3 more minutes or until golden brown.

Remove to a paper towel–lined plate to drain before serving.

Serve with sour cream.

CORN & JALAPEÑO CAKES WITH CHEDDAR SAUCE

You can pour cheese sauce over anything and I'm down for eating it. These corn and jalapeño cakes are just plain delicious. Stack 'em up, pour on some cheese, and enjoy a delicious side dish. You can adjust the amount of jalapeños to suit your taste.

Prep Time: 10 minutes
Cook Time: 10 minutes
Total Time: 20 minutes
Yield: 12 (2-inch) pancakes

For the cheese sauce:
2 Tbsp. butter
2 Tbsp. flour
¾ cup milk
1 cup grated cheddar cheese

For the pancakes:
½ cup flour
½ cup cornmeal
1 Tbsp. sugar
1 tsp. baking powder
½ tsp. salt
¾ cup buttermilk
1 egg, beaten
1 Tbsp. vegetable oil
1 cup frozen or fresh corn kernels
1 jalapeño, minced
1 Tbsp. chopped chives

To make the cheese sauce, melt the butter in a small saucepan over medium heat. Once melted, whisk in the flour and cook for 2 minutes.

Whisk in the milk and continue stirring over medium heat until it reaches the consistency of a gravy.

Remove from the heat and stir in the grated cheese. Stir until the mixture is smooth. Set aside while cooking the pancakes.

To make the pancakes, heat a large skillet or griddle over medium heat.

Whisk together the flour, cornmeal, sugar, baking powder, and salt in a medium bowl.

In a small bowl, stir together the buttermilk, egg, and oil. Add the wet ingredients to the dry and stir until just combined. Fold in the corn, jalapeño, and chives.

Use a medium cookie scoop to scoop the dough onto the griddle. Flatten slightly. Cook for 3 minutes per side or until golden brown and cooked through. Repeat with remaining pancakes.

Serve the pancakes with the cheddar cheese sauce.

ROASTED RED PEPPER & GOAT CHEESE QUINOA PATTIES

It took my family and me quite some time to jump on the quinoa bandwagon, but now that I'm serving it up more creatively, we all love it! The goat cheese lends a creamy tang to these patties, and the roasted red peppers give just a hint of sweetness and color. Biting into the crispy exterior before hitting the smooth and somewhat creamy center is the best part though.

Prep Time: 10 minutes
Cook Time: 40 minutes
Total Time: 50 minutes
Yield: 12 small patties

½ cup quinoa
1 cup chicken stock
3 ounces goat cheese
1 egg, beaten
½ cup panko bread crumbs
1 clove garlic, grated
2 Tbsp. diced roasted red pepper
1 Tbsp. chopped chives
½ tsp. salt
Oil, for frying

Add the quinoa and chicken stock to a medium saucepan and bring to a boil over medium heat. Cover, reduce heat, and continue cooking for 20 minutes, or until the liquid has been absorbed. Remove from the heat and let sit for 10 minutes.

Add the goat cheese to the warm quinoa and stir to coat. Stir in the egg, panko, garlic, red pepper, chives, and salt.

Heat a large skillet over medium-high heat and add just enough oil to cover the bottom of the pan.

When the oil is hot, use a cookie scoop to scoop out one ball of the quinoa mixture into your hands. Lightly press into a patty. Place in the hot oil. Repeat with the remaining quinoa, being sure not to overcrowd the pan. Cook for 2 minutes per side or until golden brown and crispy.

Drain on a paper towel–lined plate.

Serve warm.

SLOPPY JOE CORN CAKES

In my family, sloppy joes are always a crowd pleaser. The main problem I have with them is that I'm usually unprepared and don't have any sandwich buns in the house. I've fixed that problem by serving the sloppy joe mixture over a couple of sweet corn cakes, making this a bit less sloppy, since you'll be eating with a fork. The sloppy joe sauce in this recipe can easily be swapped out for the canned version if you're short on time, but my whole family prefers my homemade sweet and tangy sauce.

Prep Time: 10 minutes
Cook Time: 10 minutes
Total Time: 20 minutes
Yield: 4–6 servings

For the sloppy joes:
1 lb. ground beef
1 bell pepper, any color
1 cup ketchup
¼ cup water
2 Tbsp. brown sugar
2 tsp. prepared yellow mustard
2 tsp. Worcestershire sauce
½ tsp. onion powder
½ tsp. salt

For the pancakes:
½ cup flour
½ cup cornmeal
1 Tbsp. sugar
1 tsp. baking powder
½ tsp. salt
¾ cup buttermilk
1 egg, beaten
1 Tbsp. vegetable oil
1 tsp. hot pepper sauce
1 cup frozen or fresh corn kernels

To make the sloppy joes, heat a medium skillet over medium heat. Add the beef to the pan and break up with a spatula. Dice the pepper and add to the pan with the beef. Continue cooking, stirring occasionally and breaking up the meat, until cooked through and no longer pink. Drain the fat and return to the pan.

In a small bowl, combine the ketchup, water, brown sugar, mustard, Worcestershire sauce, onion powder, and salt. Stir until smooth. Pour over the ground beef, reduce heat to low, and let cook 10 minutes, stirring occasionally.

While the sloppy joes are cooking, prepare the corn cakes.

In a medium bowl, whisk together the flour, cornmeal, sugar, baking powder, and salt in a medium bowl.

In a small bowl, stir together the buttermilk, egg, oil, and hot pepper sauce. Add the wet ingredients to the dry and stir until just combined. Fold in the corn.

Use a medium cookie scoop (about 2 tablespoons) to scoop the dough onto the griddle. Flatten slightly if needed. Cook for 3 minutes per side or until golden brown and cooked through. Repeat with remaining pancakes.

To serve, place two corn cakes on each plate and top with the sloppy joe mixture.

HAM AND CHEDDAR RICE CAKES

Ham, cheddar, and rice just belong together if you ask me! I mixed them all up and fried them in a bit of oil for this easy recipe. You'll get 8 small cakes out of this, which is perfect for a side dish. If you'd like to serve them as a main dish, you might want to double the recipe, depending on how many you're feeding. They go great with a side salad!

Prep Time: 5 minutes
Cook Time: 10 minutes
Total Time: 15 minutes
Yield: 8 (2-inch) cakes

1 cup cold cooked rice
1 egg, beaten
½ cup finely diced ham
¼ cup grated cheddar cheese
¼ cup flour
¼ tsp. garlic powder
¼ tsp. salt
2 Tbsp. vegetable oil

Add the rice, egg, ham, cheese, flour, garlic powder, and salt to a medium bowl and stir to combine. The mixture should be thick and fairly sticky.

Heat the oil in a large skillet over medium heat until it shimmers. Use a medium cookie scoop or large serving spoon to scoop out the rice cakes and drop them into the oil. Gently press them to about ½-inch thick with a spatula. Cook for 3 minutes or until the bottom is golden brown.

Flip the cakes over and continue cooking for 2 more minutes or until golden brown.

Remove to a paper towel lined plate to drain the grease. Serve hot.

savory pancakes

SWEET POTATO LATKES WITH BARBECUE PULLED PORK AND COLESLAW

This dinner is always a hit with my family! We all love pulled pork sandwiches, but this open-faced version is a new favorite twist. Instead of a sandwich bun, the pork is piled high on crispy sweet potato latkes and topped with coleslaw. Topping your pork with coleslaw is a bit of a regional thing, so feel free to skip it or serve it on the side if that's more your style.

Prep Time: 30 minutes
Cook Time: 8 hours 15 minutes
Total Time: 8 hours 45 minutes
Serves: 5 servings, with leftover pork

For the pork: .
3 pound boneless pork shoulder roast
¼ cup paprika
¼ cup brown sugar
3 Tbsp. garlic powder
3 Tbsp. salt
2 Tbsp. onion powder
2 Tbsp. ground black pepper
1 Tbsp. dried parsley flakes
1 cup bottled barbecue sauce

For the latkes:
2 medium sweet potatoes
2 eggs
1 tsp. onion powder
¼ tsp. garlic powder
¼ tsp. salt
2 Tbsp. oil, for frying
Prepared coleslaw for serving

To make the pork, add the pork roast to a slow cooker. In a small bowl, combine the dry seasonings and mix well. Sprinkle the dry mixture over the pork, patting it in and turning to coat all sides.

Set the slow cooker to low and cook for 8 hours.

When the pork is done, shred the meat with two forks. Add the barbecue sauce and toss to coat.

To make the latkes, peel and wash the sweet potatoes. Grate the potatoes with a cheese grater or food processor. You'll end up with about 1½ cups of grated sweet potato.

Add the grated potato to a bowl and mix in the eggs, onion powder, garlic powder, and salt. Stir to combine.

Heat a large skillet over medium heat and add the oil to the pan. When the oil begins to shimmer, use a medium cookie scoop or large serving spoon to carefully drop the sweet potato mixture into the oil. Flatten it out a bit with the back of the spoon. Be careful not to overcrowd the pan.

Cook for 5 minutes or until golden brown. Flip and continue cooking 3 more minutes or until golden brown.

Remove to a paper towel–lined plate to drain and repeat with the remaining latkes.

To serve, spoon the pulled pork over the latkes and top with more barbecue sauce and coleslaw, if desired.

BLACK BEAN AND CORN CAKES WITH GUACAMOLE

I'm a pretty firm believer that guacamole goes with everything, but even I was a little leery of pancakes and guac. I'm not sure what I was concerned about, because these little black bean and corn cakes were made to be slathered in the green stuff!

Prep Time: 10 minutes
Cook Time: 10 minutes
Total Time: 20 minutes
Yield: 12 (2-inch) pancakes

For the guacamole:
2 Hass avocados
¼ chopped onion
1 clove garlic, minced
2 Tbsp. chopped cilantro
½ tsp. ground cumin
½ tsp. salt
Juice of half a lime

For the pancakes:
½ cup flour
½ cup cornmeal
1 tsp. sugar
1 tsp. baking powder
½ tsp. salt
¾ cup buttermilk
1 egg, beaten
1 Tbsp. vegetable oil
½ cup canned black beans
¼ cup fresh or frozen corn kernels

To make the guacamole, cut the avocados in half and scoop out the flesh into a small bowl. Add the remaining ingredients and mash with a fork.

To make the pancakes, heat a large skillet or griddle over medium heat.

Whisk together the flour, cornmeal, sugar, baking powder, and salt in a medium bowl.

In a small bowl, stir together the buttermilk, egg, and oil. Add the wet ingredients to the dry and stir until just combined. Fold in the black beans and corn.

Use a medium cookie scoop to scoop the dough onto the griddle. Flatten slightly. Cook for 3 minutes per side or until golden brown and cooked through. Repeat with remaining pancakes.

Spread with guacamole or serve on the side.

LOADED POTATO PANCAKES

Baked potatoes loaded with cheese, sour cream, and bacon are one of my favorite side dishes! I mixed everything up together and created these little bites of potato goodness.

Prep Time: 10 minutes
Cook Time: 10 minutes
Total Time: 20 minutes
Yield: 10 (3-inch) pancakes

2 cups cold mashed potatoes
3 strips bacon, fried and crumbled
1 egg, beaten
2 tablespoons sour cream, plus more for serving
1 cup grated cheddar cheese
1 cup flour, divided
2 tablespoons diced green onions
1 teaspoon salt
½ teaspoon ground black pepper
Vegetable oil, for frying

In a large bowl, combine the mashed potatoes, crumbled bacon, egg, sour cream, cheddar cheese, ⅓ cup flour, salt, and pepper. Stir until just combined. The mixture should be fairly sticky, but workable. Check the dough by grabbing a small handful and rolling into a ball. If the mixture is too difficult to work with, add more flour, one tablespoon at a time, until the mixture is just easy enough to work with.

Place a large skillet over medium heat and pour in just enough oil to fully cover the bottom of the pan.

Add the remaining flour to a small bowl.

Use your hands to scoop out a golf ball–sized amount of dough, roll into a ball, roll in the flour, and then flatten into a patty. Set aside and repeat with the remaining potato mixture.

When the oil is hot, add the pancakes in batches to the skillet and cook for 2–3 minutes per side, or until golden brown.

Serve with extra sour cream.

DESSERT
pancakes

♡♡♡♡♡♡♡♡♡♡♡♡♡♡♡♡

When you think about it, a pan-cake is just a small cake cooked on the stovetop instead of baked in the oven, which means that pancakes make an excellent dessert! Not only that, but they're quick and simple to throw together at the last minute, and you don't need to heat up the oven.

♡♡♡♡♡♡♡♡♡♡♡♡♡♡♡♡

ROASTED S'MORES PANCAKES

Who needs a campfire? As long as you have a griddle and a hot oven, you can bring the campfire inside with these Roasted S'mores Pancakes! The graham cracker crumbs get incorporated right into the pancake batter, giving them a unique flavor, and the toasty marshmallows on top just bring everything together perfectly!

Prep Time: 10 minutes
Cook Time: 10 minutes
Total Time: 20 minutes
Yield: 7 (4-inch) pancakes

⅔ cup graham cracker crumbs (from 4 whole crackers)
½ cup flour
2 Tbsp. sugar
1 tsp. baking powder
½ tsp. baking soda
¼ tsp. salt
¾ cup buttermilk
1 egg, beaten
2 Tbsp. vegetable oil
1 tsp. vanilla extract
1 cup mini marshmallows
Chocolate Syrup, page 143

Heat a large skillet or griddle over medium heat.

In a medium bowl, combine the graham cracker crumbs, flour, sugar, baking powder, baking soda, and salt. Whisk to combine.

In a small bowl, mix together the buttermilk, egg, oil, and vanilla.

Stir the wet ingredients into the dry ingredients until combined but still slightly lumpy.

Spray your cooking surface with nonstick cooking spray and place ¼ cup of the pancake batter in the pan. Cook for 3 minutes per side or until cooked through. Repeat with remaining pancakes.

While the pancakes are cooking, spread the marshmallows out on a foil-lined baking sheet and turn your oven to broil. Place the marshmallows under the broiler for one minute, keeping a close eye on them. They can go from perfect to burnt in seconds, so do keep a close watch. Remove from the oven when golden brown on top. Slide a large spatula under the marshmallows and carefully transfer them from the sheet pan to the top of the pancakes. Alternatively, use a kitchen torch to roast the tops of the marshmallows.

Top your pancakes with the chocolate syrup.

CHOCOLATE PEANUT BUTTER CUP PANCAKES

I've spent my entire life as a devout chocolate peanut butter cup addict. I can never get enough of those little candies, and now I've gone and added them to pancakes. These pancakes are just a little over the top and ridiculous, which is what I love most about them.

Prep Time: 5 minutes
Cook Time: 10 minutes
Total Time: 15 minutes
Yield: 8 (4-inch) pancakes

For the pancakes:
1 cup flour
2 Tbsp. sugar
1 tsp. baking powder
½ tsp. baking soda
¼ tsp. salt
1¼ cup buttermilk
1 egg, beaten

For the topping:
⅓ cup creamy peanut butter
½ cup mini chocolate peanut butter cups, chopped into small pieces
Chocolate Syrup, page 143
Whipped Cream, for serving

Heat a large skillet or griddle over medium heat.

In a medium bowl, combine the flour, sugar, baking powder, baking soda, and salt. Whisk to combine.

In a small bowl, mix together the buttermilk, egg, and peanut butter.

Stir the wet ingredients into the dry ingredients until combined but still slightly lumpy.

Spray your cooking surface with nonstick cooking spray and place ¼ cup of the pancake batter in the pan. The batter will be very thick, and you will need to spread it a bit with the back of a spoon, spatula, or your ¼-cup measurer. Sprinkle immediately with a few pieces of chopped peanut butter cups. Use a spoon to spread a bit of the batter over the candy pieces. Cook for 3 minutes per side or until cooked through. Repeat with remaining pancakes.

Top with whipped cream, chocolate syrup, and more candy pieces.

CHOCOLATE PEANUT BUTTER CUP PANCAKES

COOKIES AND CREAM PANCAKES

We're obsessed with cookies and cream in this house! Whether it's just a package of chocolate sandwich cookies or ice cream loaded with soft cookies and cream, we eat it like it's going out of style. We believe that the filling is the best part, so I've loaded these pancakes up with a sweet white frosting and sprinkled crushed cookies over the top.

Prep Time: 5 minutes
Cook Time: 10 minutes
Total Time: 15 minutes
Yield: 8 (4-inch) pancakes

For the pancakes:

1 cup flour
3 Tbsp. cocoa powder
2 Tbsp. sugar
1 tsp. baking powder
½ tsp. baking soda
¼ tsp. salt
½ cup chopped chocolate sandwich cookies, divided
1 cup buttermilk
1 egg, beaten
2 Tbsp. vegetable oil
2 Tbsp. chocolate syrup on page 143
1 tsp. vanilla extract

For the filling:

8 Tbsp. butter, room temperature
1 tsp. vanilla extract
¼ tsp. salt
2 cups powdered sugar
¼ cup heavy whipping cream

To make the pancakes, heat the griddle or skillet over medium heat.

In a medium bowl, combine the flour, cocoa powder, sugar, baking powder, baking soda, and salt. Mix in ¼ cup of the chocolate cookie crumbles. Whisk to combine.

In a small bowl, mix together the buttermilk, egg, oil, chocolate syrup, and vanilla.

Stir the wet ingredients into the dry ingredients until combined but still slightly lumpy.

Spray your cooking surface with nonstick cooking spray and place ¼ cup of the pancake batter in the pan. Cook for 2–3 minutes and then flip and continue cooking until cooked through. Repeat with remaining pancakes.

To make the filling, beat together the butter and vanilla with an electric mixer until creamy. Gradually beat in the salt and powdered sugar until well combined. Add the heavy cream, a little at a time, to reach the consistency you desire.

Spread frosting on the pancakes, sprinkle with the remaining chopped cookies, and serve.

DOUBLE CHOCOLATE
SALTED CARAMEL PANCAKES

Chocolate cake with caramel frosting is always a favorite dessert, and I thought it'd make a great pancake too! It's so much simpler to make a stack of pancakes than an entire cake, and you don't even have to heat up the oven. The fact that you're just 20 minutes away from this easy dessert is a bit dangerous, but I think you can handle it!

Prep Time: 10 minutes
Cook Time: 10 minutes
Total Time: 20 minutes
Yield: 8 (4-inch) pancakes

1 cup flour
3 Tbsp. cocoa powder
2 Tbsp. sugar
1 tsp. baking powder
½ tsp. baking soda
¼ tsp. salt
1 cup buttermilk
1 egg, beaten
2 Tbsp. vegetable oil
1 tsp. vanilla extract
½ cup dark chocolate chips
Salted Caramel Syrup on page 148

Heat a large skillet or griddle over medium heat.

In a medium bowl, combine the flour, cocoa powder, sugar, baking powder, baking soda, and salt. Whisk to combine.

In a small bowl, mix together the buttermilk, egg, oil, and vanilla.

Stir the wet ingredients into the dry ingredients until combined but still slightly lumpy.

Pour ¼ cup of batter onto a heated griddle or skillet. Sprinkle a few chocolate chips over the batter. Cook for 3 minutes or until bubbles have formed on the surface and have popped. Flip the pancakes and continue cooking until cooked through.

Repeat with remaining batter.

Top with the Salted Caramel Syrup on page 148.

RAINBOW PANCAKES WITH FLUFFY FROSTING

These rainbow pancakes cheer you up just by looking at them, don't they? I'm addicted to color, and these don't disappoint! There are a couple of options for making these. You can choose your favorite flavor and make them all one color. Alternatively, as I've shown in the picture, you can go for a rainbow of colors with multiple boxes of flavored gelatin. Either way, these will take on a slight flavor and a bright color from the gelatin, and they will bring happiness to your dining table. The color of your pancakes will vary depending on the brand and flavor of gelatin you use. You can also sneak in a bit of food coloring to up the colors, if desired.

Prep Time: 10 minutes
Cook Time: 10 minutes
Total Time: 20 minutes
Yield: 16 (4-inch) pancakes

For the pancakes:
2 cups flour
2 Tbsp. sugar
2 tsp. baking powder
1 tsp. baking soda
½ tsp. salt
2 cups buttermilk
2 eggs, beaten
¼ cup vegetable oil
1 tsp. vanilla extract
¼ cup flavored gelatin powder, all from one box, or 2 teaspoons each from 6 different colored boxes

For the frosting:
8 Tbsp. butter, room temperature
1 tsp. vanilla extract
¼ tsp. salt
2 cups powdered sugar
¼ cup heavy whipping cream

Heat a large skillet or griddle over medium heat.

In a medium bowl, combine the flour, sugar, baking powder, baking soda, and salt. Whisk to combine.

In a small bowl, mix together the buttermilk, eggs, oil, and vanilla.

Stir the wet ingredients into the dry ingredients until combined but still slightly lumpy.

If you're making one color and flavor of pancakes, stir the ¼ cup of gelatin powder into the pancake mix.

If you're making rainbow pancakes, place a scant ½ cup of batter into 6 separate bowls. Stir 2 teaspoons of one flavor of gelatin powder into one bowl. Repeat with the remaining flavors and colors.

Spray your cooking surface with nonstick cooking spray and place ¼ cup of the pancake batter in the pan.

Cook for 3 minutes per side or until cooked through. Repeat with remaining pancakes.

To make the frosting, beat together the butter and vanilla with an electric mixer until creamy. Gradually beat in the salt and powdered sugar until well combined. Add the heavy cream, a little at a time, to reach the consistency you desire.

Spread frosting on the pancakes and serve.

CHEESECAKE PANCAKES

I've been hooked on cheesecake ever since my high-school-boyfriend-turned-husband insisted that we make a no-bake cheesecake from a box mix once. It was divine. Not long after that, I worked up the courage to make a real, from-scratch cheesecake, and life hasn't been the same since. I wanted to incorporate that tangy flavor and the luscious creaminess of a real cheesecake into these pancakes, and I think I did so quite nicely. Bonus points: Using pudding mix as the flavoring makes these super easy to prepare!

Prep Time: 10 minutes
Cook Time: 10 minutes
Total Time: 20 minutes
Yield: 8 (4-inch) pancakes

For the pancakes:
¾ cup flour
¼ cup cheesecake-flavored pudding mix
1 Tbsp. sugar
1 tsp. baking powder
½ tsp. baking soda
¼ tsp salt
1 cup buttermilk
1 egg, beaten
2 Tbsp. vegetable oil

For the frosting:
4 oz. butter, room temperature
4 oz. cream cheese, room temperature
¾ cup powdered sugar
2 Tbsp. cheesecake-flavored pudding mix
1 Tbsp. milk
1 graham cracker, crumbled

Heat a large skillet or griddle over medium heat.

In a medium bowl, combine the flour, pudding mix, sugar, baking powder, baking soda, and salt. Whisk to combine.

In a small bowl, mix together the buttermilk, egg, and oil.

Stir the wet ingredients into the dry ingredients until combined but still slightly lumpy.

Spray your cooking surface with nonstick cooking spray and place ¼ cup of the pancake batter in the pan. Swirl a spoon over the top of the batter to spread it a bit, because this batter is very thick. Cook for 3 minutes per side or until cooked through. Repeat with remaining pancakes.

While pancakes are cooking, beat together the butter and cream cheese with an electric mixer on medium speed until light and fluffy.

Beat in the powdered sugar, pudding mix, and milk until well combined.

Spread the frosting on the pancakes, stack, and sprinkle with the crumbled graham cracker.

Variations: Try topping these with your favorite berry for a decadent dessert with a burst of fruity flavor. Strawberries are my favorite!

PECAN PIE PANCAKES

I'm sticking these Pecan Pie Pancakes in the "desserts" chapter because, after all . . . pie is dessert. The thing is, I could and would (and totally do) eat these for breakfast. The gooey pecan topping is just sweet enough to call these a dessert, but you go ahead and eat them whenever the mood strikes.

Prep Time: 5 minutes
Cook Time: 15 minutes
Total Time: 20 minutes
Yield: 6 (4-inch) pancakes

For the pancakes:
1 cup flour
2 Tbsp. sugar
1 tsp. baking powder
½ tsp. baking soda
½ tsp. ground cinnamon
¼ tsp. salt
1 cup buttermilk
1 egg, beaten
2 Tbsp. vegetable oil
½ tsp. vanilla extract

For the pecan pie topping:
¼ cup butter
¼ cup corn syrup
¼ cup brown sugar
¼ cup maple syrup
1 cup chopped pecans
Dash of salt

Heat a large skillet or griddle over medium heat.

In a medium bowl, combine the flour, sugar, baking powder, baking soda, cinnamon, and salt. Whisk to combine.

In a small bowl, mix together the buttermilk, egg, oil, and vanilla.

Stir the wet ingredients into the dry ingredients until combined but still slightly lumpy.

Spray your cooking surface with nonstick cooking spray and place ¼ cup of the pancake batter in the pan. Cook for 3 minutes per side or until cooked through. Repeat with remaining pancakes.

While the pancakes are cooking, add the pecan pie topping ingredients to a small saucepan set over medium-low heat. Stir the mixture until the butter melts and the pecans are coated. Bring to a boil, stirring occasionally, and then remove from the heat.

Immediately pour the topping over the pancakes. It will thicken up a bit as it cools, so it's best to serve warm.

CHOCOLATE CHIP COOKIE DOUGH PANCAKES

Raise your hand if you've ever made cookies just because you really needed a spoonful or two of the unbaked dough. (My hand is waving around in the air like a maniac.) These pancakes are full of cookie dough, and it stays perfectly gooey and melty in the pancake, creating an outrageous dessert. I serve these just as they are, but feel free to top them with some chocolate syrup and pecans, if you'd like.

Prep Time: 15 minutes
Cook Time: 10 minutes
Total Time: 25 minutes
Yield: 8 (4-inch) pancakes

For the cookie dough:
½ cup butter, room temperature
½ cup brown sugar
1 tsp. vanilla extract
1 cup flour
2 Tbsp. milk
¼ cup mini chocolate chips

For the pancakes:
1 cup flour
2 Tbsp. brown sugar
1 tsp. baking powder
½ tsp. baking soda
¼ tsp. salt
1 cup buttermilk
1 egg, beaten
2 Tbsp. melted butter
1 tsp. vanilla extract
¼ cup mini chocolate chips

To prepare the cookie dough, place the butter and brown sugar in a medium mixing bowl and beat with an electric mixer until light and fluffy. Beat in the vanilla extract.

Stir in the flour and milk and beat until mixture is well combined.

Stir in the chocolate chips.

Roll the cookie dough into 24 balls, each about 1 teaspoon's worth of dough. Set aside.

To make the pancakes, heat the griddle or skillet over medium heat.

In a medium bowl, combine the flour, sugar, baking powder, baking soda, and salt. Whisk to combine.

In a small bowl, mix together the buttermilk, egg, melted butter, and vanilla.

Stir the wet ingredients into the dry ingredients until combined but still slightly lumpy. Gently fold in the mini chocolate chips.

Spray your cooking surface with nonstick cooking spray and place ¼ cup of the pancake batter in the pan. Add 3 balls of cookie dough to the top of each pancake. Cook for 2–3 minutes and then flip and continue cooking until cooked through. Repeat with remaining pancakes.

BETTER THAN ANYTHING PANCAKES

You know the cake I'm talking about, right? Better Than Anything Cake, Better Than Sex Cake, Quilt Cake, Poke Cake . . . it has a lot of names, but mostly people are too busy shoving each little bite in their face to worry about settling on one specific name. These fudgy pancakes are every bit as decadent as the cake they're inspired by! These are rich, and I find that a stack of two pancakes makes a perfect serving size, but feel free to adjust as you see fit.

Prep Time: 5 minutes
Cook Time: 10 minutes
Total Time: 15 minutes
Yield: 8 (4-inch) pancakes

For the pancakes:
1 cup flour
3 Tbsp. cocoa powder
2 Tbsp. sugar
1 tsp. baking powder
½ tsp. baking soda
¼ tsp. salt
1 cup buttermilk
1 egg, beaten
2 Tbsp. vegetable oil
2 Tbsp. chocolate syrup on page 143
1 tsp. vanilla extract

For the topping:
2 Tbsp. sweetened condensed milk
2 Tbsp. caramel ice cream topping
Fresh whipped cream, for topping
2 Tbsp. chocolate-covered toffee pieces

To make the pancakes, heat the griddle or skillet over medium heat.

In a medium bowl, combine the flour, cocoa powder, sugar, baking powder, baking soda, and salt. Whisk to combine.

In a small bowl, mix together the buttermilk, egg, oil, chocolate syrup, and vanilla.

Stir the wet ingredients into the dry ingredients until combined but still slightly lumpy.

Spray your cooking surface with nonstick cooking spray and place ¼ cup of the pancake batter in the pan. Cook for 2–3 minutes, and then flip and continue cooking until cooked through. Repeat with remaining pancakes.

In a small bowl, stir together the sweetened condensed milk and caramel ice cream topping. Spread about 1 teaspoon of the caramel mixture on each pancake. Stack the pancakes by twos, top with whipped cream, and sprinkle on toffee pieces.

dessert pancakes

129

BIRTHDAY CAKE PANCAKES

Special days mean special breakfasts in my house! The kids love waking up to a celebration, and these birthday cake pancakes are just that. They're full of the flavor of birthday cake, loaded with sprinkles, and topped with a sweet glaze and even more sprinkles. These are definitely sweet and make a great dessert, especially if the celebration is just for one or two and you can't eat an entire cake!

Prep Time: 5 minutes
Cook Time: 10 minutes
Total Time: 15 minutes
Yield: 8 (4-inch) pancakes

For the pancakes:
½ cup flour
½ cup dry boxed yellow cake mix
1 tsp. baking powder
½ tsp. baking soda
⅛ tsp. salt
1 cup buttermilk
1 egg, beaten
2 Tbsp. vegetable oil
½ tsp. vanilla extract
¼ cup sprinkles

For the glaze:
1 cup powdered sugar
6 Tbsp. heavy whipping cream
¼ cup sprinkles

Heat a large skillet or griddle over medium heat.

In a medium bowl, combine the flour, cake mix, baking powder, baking soda, and salt. Whisk to combine.

In a small bowl, mix together the buttermilk, egg, oil, and vanilla.

Stir the wet ingredients into the dry ingredients until combined, but still slightly lumpy.

Gently stir in the sprinkles.

Spray your cooking surface with nonstick cooking spray and place ¼ cup of the pancake batter in the pan. Cook for 2–3 minutes, and then flip and continue cooking until cooked through. Repeat with remaining pancakes.

To make the glaze, whisk together the powdered sugar and whipping cream in a small bowl until smooth.

Pour the glaze over the pancakes, and then top with extra sprinkles.

CARROT CAKE PANCAKES WITH CREAM CHEESE FROSTING

My husband is a cake hater. It shocks me each time I bake a cake and offer him a piece, because what is there to dislike about cake? Luckily, he will happily eat carrot cake, which is strange since he's a bit of a veggie hater as well. Either way, he likes carrot cake and I like him, so these pancakes had to happen.

Prep Time: 10 minutes
Cook Time: 10 minutes
Total Time: 20 minutes
Yield: 8 (4-inch) pancakes

For the pancakes:
1 cup flour
2 Tbsp. brown sugar
1 tsp. ground cinnamon
1 tsp. baking powder
½ tsp. baking soda
½ tsp. salt
¾ cup buttermilk
¼ cup carrot purée
1 egg, beaten
1 Tbsp. vegetable oil
1 tsp. vanilla extract

For the frosting:
4 oz. cream cheese, room temperature
4 oz. butter, room temperature
¾ cup powdered sugar
1 Tbsp. milk
½ tsp. vanilla

Heat a large skillet or griddle over medium heat.

In a medium bowl, combine the flour, sugar, cinnamon, baking powder, baking soda, and salt. Whisk to combine.

In a small bowl, mix together the buttermilk, carrot purée, egg, oil, and vanilla.

Stir the wet ingredients into the dry ingredients until combined but still slightly lumpy.

Spray your cooking surface with nonstick cooking spray and place ¼ cup of the pancake batter in the pan. Cook for 3 minutes per side or until cooked through. Repeat with remaining pancakes.

To make the frosting, beat together the cream cheese and butter until smooth. Beat in the powdered sugar, milk, and vanilla. Spread over the warm pancakes.

PINEAPPLE UPSIDE-DOWN CAKE PANCAKES

Pineapple Upside-Down Cake is a classic, and now it's made even easier in the form of pancakes! These whip up really quickly and have all the traditional flavors of your favorite fruity cake.

Prep Time: 5 minutes
Cook Time: 10 minutes
Total Time: 15 minutes
Yield: 8 (4-inch) pancakes

For the pancakes:
½ cup flour
½ cup dry boxed yellow cake mix
1 tsp. baking powder
½ tsp. baking soda
⅛ tsp. salt
1 cup buttermilk
1 egg, beaten
2 Tbsp. vegetable oil
½ tsp. vanilla extract

For the topping:
8 sliced pineapple rings from a can
8 maraschino cherries, stems removed
Salted Caramel Syrup for serving, page 148

Heat a large skillet or griddle over medium heat.

In a medium bowl, combine the flour, cake mix, baking powder, baking soda, and salt. Whisk to combine.

In a small bowl, mix together the buttermilk, egg, oil, and vanilla.

Stir the wet ingredients into the dry ingredients until combined but still slightly lumpy.

Spray your cooking surface with nonstick cooking spray and place ¼ cup of the pancake batter in the pan. Immediately place a pineapple ring in the center of the pancake and gently press down. Place a cherry in the center of the pineapple and press down. Cook for 2–3 minutes or until bubbles form and pop on the surface, and then flip and continue cooking until cooked through. Repeat with remaining pancakes.

Serve with the caramel syrup from page 148.

SAUCES AND *syrups*

I love maple syrup just as much as the next girl (the real stuff, please. None of that fake syrup for me!), but sometimes you just have to add a little variety to your pancakes! Many of these toppings work equally well atop ice cream, brownies, cheesecakes, spoons, and fingers!

STRAWBERRY SYRUP

This fresh syrup is bursting with the flavor of juicy, ripe strawberries. It's perfect on pancakes, but don't forget to stir some into your glass of milk, drizzle it over ice cream, or spread it on top of cheesecake.

Prep Time: 5 minutes
Cook Time: 10 minutes
Total Time: 15 minutes
Yield: ½ cup

---

1 cup halved strawberries
¾ cup sugar
⅓ cup water
1 Tbsp. butter
½ tsp. vanilla extract

Add the strawberries, sugar, and water to a small saucepan and turn the heat to medium-low. Bring to a boil, stirring occasionally.

Remove mixture to a blender or use an immersion blender and blend until smooth.

Return to the saucepan over low heat and cook for 10 more minutes, stirring occasionally.

Remove from heat and stir in the butter and vanilla.

Store (covered) in the refrigerator for up to 2 weeks.

BROWNED BUTTER DRIZZLE

Goodness, I'm not even sure where to begin with this browned butter drizzle. If you haven't experimented with browned butter yet, then you really need to start! We all know that butter is delicious, but browning it in a saucepan completely transforms it. Drizzle this over rice crispy treats the next time you make them, but be prepared to never enjoy another plain crispy treat again!

Prep Time: 3 minutes
Cook Time: 5 minutes
Total Time: 8 minutes
Yield: ½ cup

½ cup butter
1¼ cups powdered sugar

Add the butter to a small saucepan over medium heat and let melt. Once melted, continue cooking, whisking often, until the butter foams. When the butter begins foaming, whisk constantly until the butter turns a deep golden shade. Remove from the heat and whisk in the powdered sugar.

Use immediately or store in the refrigerator for up to 2 weeks. Reheat before serving.

CHOCOLATE SYRUP

This rich chocolate syrup tastes really similar to the squeeze bottles you'd find in the store, but it doesn't have any of the strange ingredients. It's simple to make, lasts in the fridge for a month, and has so many uses! I like to just dip my finger in and lick it off, but it's good on pancakes, ice cream, and other desserts too.

Prep Time: 2 minutes
Cook Time: 8 minutes
Total Time: 10 minutes
Yield: 1 cup

¾ cup water
1 cup sugar
¾ cup cocoa powder
¼ cup light corn syrup
1 teaspoon vanilla extract

Add the water and sugar to a small sauce pan and bring to a boil.

Whisk in the cocoa powder and corn syrup and continue boiling for 3 minutes.

Remove from the heat and whisk in the vanilla extract. Let cool completely.

Store covered in the fridge for up to one month.

STRAWBERRY RHUBARB SYRUP

Every Spring I look forward to the colorful bunches of rhubarb at the farmers' markets and grocery stores. This brightly colored syrup reminds me of the pie my mama used to make every Spring, and I can never get enough.

Prep Time: 10 minutes
Cook Time: 40 minutes
Total Time: 50 minutes
Yield: ¾ cup syrup

2 cups chopped rhubarb, fresh or frozen
2 cups chopped strawberries, fresh or frozen
1 cup water
1 cup sugar
1 tsp. vanilla extract

Add everything but the vanilla extract to a medium saucepan set over medium heat. Bring to a boil, reduce to a simmer, and cook for 20 minutes, stirring occasionally.

Remove the mixture to a fine mesh strainer and drain the juice into a bowl. Press on the fruit with the back of a spoon to extract as much liquid as possible. You should end up with about 1½ cups of liquid.

Discard the solids and rinse out the saucepan. Return the liquid to the saucepan and return to a low boil. Continue cooking for about 20 minutes or until the liquid has reduced to about ¾ of a cup.

Cool before serving. Store in a covered container in the refrigerator for up to 2 weeks.

Tip: If rhubarb is not in season, check your grocer's freezer section. I'm often lucky enough to find it next to the other frozen fruits.

MAPLE GLAZE

The only way to improve maple syrup is to turn it into a thick, sweet glaze that crusts over as it hardens. Try it over ice cream for a special treat.

Prep Time: 5 minutes
Total Time: 5 minutes
Yield: 1 cup glaze

3 Tbsp. melted butter
½ cup maple syrup
1½ cups powdered sugar

Add the melted butter and syrup to a medium-sized bowl. Sift the powdered sugar into the bowl and whisk to combine.

Serve immediately, because the glaze will start to harden.

Store in the fridge in a covered dish for up to 1 week. Heat in the microwave until pourable and stir before serving.

SALTED CARAMEL SYRUP

It seems like salted caramel is all the rage these days, and I couldn't be happier about it! There is just something so perfect about sweet caramel dotted with flecks of salt. This syrup works great on your pancakes, of course, but don't limit its use. It easily replaces that jarred ice cream topping many of us buy, and it's amazing drizzled in a cup of coffee.

Prep Time: 5 minutes
Cook Time: 5 minutes
Total Time: 10 minutes
Yield: 1 cup

½ cup butter
1 cup sugar
1 tsp. lemon juice
¾ cup heavy whipping cream
1 tsp. vanilla
½ tsp. kosher salt

Melt the butter in a medium saucepan over medium heat. Whisk in the sugar and lemon juice and continue whisking until the mixture turns a caramel color (about 5 minutes). Carefully whisk in the heavy cream. It will bubble up, but continue whisking until the mixture comes together (about 2 more minutes). Stir in the vanilla and salt. Allow to cool 10 minutes before serving.

Store in a covered container in the refrigerator for up to 2 weeks. Heat in the microwave to serve again.

CINNAMON SYRUP

Whether you use this cinnamon syrup for pancakes, waffles, ice cream, or to drizzle over your apple pie, you really don't want to skip this recipe! It's ready in less than 20 minutes and really packs a flavorful punch.

Prep Time: 1 minute
Cook Time: 15 minutes
Total Time: 16 minutes
Yield: ¾ cup syrup

---

1 cup brown sugar
1 teaspoon ground cinnamon
2 tsp. cornstarch
1 cup cool water
2 Tbsp. butter
1 tsp. vanilla extract

Add the brown sugar and cinnamon in a small saucepan and stir to combine.

Dissolve the cornstarch in the cup of water by whisking until smooth.

Whisk the liquid into the brown sugar mixture, and turn the heat to medium.

Cook, whisking frequently, until mixture comes to a rolling boil. Continue cooking, whisking occasionally, for about 10 minutes or until the mixture has thickened a bit.

Remove from the heat and stir in the butter and vanilla extract. Whisk until smooth and shiny.

Serve warm.

Store in a covered container in the refrigerator for up to 2 weeks. Heat in the microwave before using again.

sauces and syrups

APPLE CIDER SYRUP

This tart syrup is chock full of flavor. Thick, sweet, and sticky, I love this poured over any pancake, but it goes best with the Apple Cider Pancakes featured on page 6. It has a very strong, somewhat tart flavor that I can't get enough of.

Prep Time: 1 minute
Cook Time: 20 minutes
Total Time: 21 minutes
Yield: 1 cup syrup

2 cups apple cider
¾ cup brown sugar
½ tsp. ground cinnamon
⅛ tsp. ground nutmeg
2 Tbsp. butter

Add everything but the butter to a medium saucepan and bring to a boil over medium heat. Continue cooking, stirring occasionally, until the syrup has reduced by half (about 15 minutes). Stir in the butter until melted.

Mixture will thicken as it cools.

BUTTERMILK SYRUP

If you've never had buttermilk syrup before, you're probably wondering just what it is. Well, I can tell you that it's shockingly good. Sweet and thick, it reminds me a bit of caramel sauce. My kids prefer this to regular maple syrup, and since it's so easy to make, I don't mind a bit.

Prep Time: 5 minutes
Cook Time: 5 minutes
Total Time: 10 minutes
Yield: 1 cup syrup

½ cup butter
½ cup buttermilk
1 cup loosely packed brown sugar
½ tsp. baking soda
1 tsp. vanilla extract

Add the butter, buttermilk, and brown sugar to a medium saucepan over medium heat. Cook until the butter has melted and the sugar has dissolved, stirring frequently.

Remove from the heat and whisk in the baking soda and vanilla.

Serve warm.

Store covered in the fridge for up to 1 week.

sauces and syrups

155

CINNAMON HONEY BUTTER

This butter is always a favorite with my family. We like it on dinner rolls, biscuits, and, of course, pancakes! I skip the syrup when I'm smearing this on my pancakes because the honey sweetens everything up perfectly. I prefer to use a raw honey for this, but any good-quality honey will work.

Prep Time: 5 minutes
Total Time: 5 minutes
Yield: ½ cup butter

½ cup salted butter, room temperature
2 Tbsp. good quality honey
½ tsp. ground cinnamon

Combine all of the ingredients in a medium bowl. Beat with a mixer until well combined. Serve at room temperature.

Store, covered, in the refrigerator for up to 2 weeks.

BLUEBERRY MAPLE SYRUP

Warm maple syrup and mashed blueberries go hand in hand. This is such a simple way to dress up a stack of pancakes! You can swap in just about any berry you like.

Prep Time: 1 minutes
Cook Time: 10 minutes
Total Time: 11 minutes
Yield: 1 cup syrup

2 cups blueberries, rinsed and dried
½ cup maple syrup
¼ tsp. ground cinnamon

Add all of the ingredients to a small saucepan set over medium heat. Bring to a boil, remove from heat, and use a potato masher to mash the blueberries to your desired consistency.

Serve warm.

Store in the fridge for up to 2 weeks.

PEANUT BUTTER MAPLE SYRUP

When my husband and I were first married, it was pretty common for us to eat toaster waffles topped with peanut butter and pancake syrup for a quick breakfast or midnight snack. I figured that the only way to improve upon that would be melting real maple syrup with peanut butter and adding a splash of vanilla.

Prep Time: 1 minute
Cook Time: 5 minutes
Total Time: 6 minutes
Yield: 1 cup syrup

1 cup maple syrup
⅔ cup peanut butter
½ tsp. vanilla

Add the syrup and peanut butter to a small saucepan over low heat. Stir until the peanut butter has melted and the mixture is smooth. Remove from the heat and stir in the vanilla.

Store in the refrigerator for up to 2 weeks. Warm on the stove over low heat before serving.

RASPBERRY FRUIT BUTTER

Fresh berries and butter are two of my favorite foods, so it's only natural for me to combine them! This fruit butter is a great way to dress up pancakes and can be made with any type of berry you please. I like the tartness of the raspberries myself!

Prep Time: 5 minutes
Total Time: 5 minutes
Yield: ½ cup butter

½ cup butter, room temperature
½ cup fresh raspberries
1 Tbsp. powdered sugar

In a medium bowl, stir together the butter, raspberries, and powdered sugar until well combined, being sure to break up the berries as you stir.

Serve immediately or store in the refrigerator for up to 5 days.

COOKING MEASUREMENT EQUIVALENTS

Cups	Tablespoons	Fluid Ounces
⅛ cup	2 Tbsp.	1 fl. oz.
¼ cup	4 Tbsp.	2 fl. oz.
⅓ cup	5 Tbsp. + 1 tsp.	
½ cup	8 Tbsp.	4 fl. oz.
⅔ cup	10 Tbsp. + 2 tsp.	
¾ cup	12 Tbsp.	6 fl. oz.
1 cup	16 Tbsp.	8 fl. oz.

Cups	Fluid Ounces	Pints/Quarts/Gallons
1 cup	8 fl. oz.	½ pint
2 cups	16 fl. oz.	1 pint = ½ quart
3 cups	24 fl. oz.	1½ pints
4 cups	32 fl. oz.	2 pints = 1 quart
8 cups	64 fl. oz.	2 quarts = ½ gallon
16 cups	128 fl. oz.	4 quarts = 1 gallon

Other Helpful Equivalents

1 Tbsp.	3 tsp.
8 oz.	½ lb.
16 oz.	1 lb.

METRIC MEASUREMENT EQUIVALENTS

Approximate Weight Equivalents

Ounces	Pounds	Grams
4 oz.	¼ lb.	113 g
5 oz.		142 g
6 oz.		170 g
8 oz.	½ lb.	227 g
9 oz.		255 g
12 oz.	¾ lb.	340 g
16 oz.	1 lb.	454 g

Approximate Volume Equivalents

Cups	US Fluid Ounces	Milliliters
⅛ cup	1 fl. oz.	30 ml
¼ cup	2 fl. oz.	59 ml
½ cup	4 fl. oz.	118 ml
¾ cup	6 fl. oz.	177 ml
1 cup	8 fl. oz.	237 ml

Other Helpful Equivalents

½ tsp.	2½ ml
1 tsp.	5 ml
1 Tbsp.	15 ml

INDEX

A

Apple Cider Pancakes with Apple Cider Syrup 6
Apple Cider Syrup 152
Apple Cinnamon Oatmeal Pancakes 59
Applesauce Pancakes 55

B

Better Than Anything Pancakes 129
Birthday Cake Pancakes 130
Black Bean and Corn Cakes with Guacamole 105
BLT Potato Pancakes 89
Blueberry Almond Butter Pancakes 56
Blueberry Coconut Quinoa Pancakes 74
Blueberry Granola Crunch Pancakes 9
Blueberry Greek Yogurt Pancakes 78
Blueberry Maple Syrup 159
Breakfast Sandwiches 37
Browned Butter Drizzle 140
Brown Sugar Pancakes with Cinnamon Streusel 46
Buttermilk Syrup 155

C

Caramel Apple Pancakes 16
Carrot Cake Pancakes with Cream Cheese Frosting 133
Cheesecake Pancakes 122
Chocolate Chip Cookie Dough Pancakes 126
Chocolate Peanut Butter Cup Pancakes 112
Chocolate Strawberry Skewers 20
Chocolate Syrup 143
Cinnamon Honey Butter 156
Cinnamon Raisin Bread Pancakes 60
Cinnamon Roll Pancakes 49
Cinnamon Sugar Donut Pancakes 34
Cinnamon Syrup 151
Cookies and Cream Pancakes 117
Corn & Jalapeño Cakes with Cheddar Sauce 94

D

Double Chocolate Banana Pancakes 13
Double Chocolate Salted Caramel Pancakes 118

E

Elvis Pancakes 5

F

French Toast Pancakes 38

G

Garlic & Dill Cauliflower Cakes 93
Garlic Parmesan Zucchini Cakes 86
Glazed Donut Pancakes 42

H

Ham and Cheddar Rice Cakes 101
Hoecakes 33
Honey Bun Pancakes 45

L

Lemon Flaxseed Pancakes 73
Loaded Potato Pancakes 106

M

Maple Glaze 147
Maple-Glazed Bacon Pancakes 28
Matcha Pancakes 52

O

Orange Vanilla Pancakes with Vanilla Maple Syrup 25
Oven-Fried Chicken and Pancakes 83

P

Peach Pecan Pancakes 2
Peanut Butter & Jelly Pancakes 41
Peanut Butter Maple Syrup 160
Pecan Pie Pancakes 125
Pineapple Upside-Down Cake Pancakes 134
Pumpkin Pancakes with Browned Butter Drizzle 10
Pumpkin Quinoa Cakes 77

R

Rainbow Pancakes with Fluffy Frosting 121
Raspberry Cookie Butter Pancakes 19
Raspberry Fruit Butter 163
Roasted Red Pepper & Goat Cheese Quinoa Patties 97
Roasted S'mores Pancakes 111

S

Salted Caramel Syrup 148
Sloppy Joe Corn Cakes 98
Strawberry Rhubarb Syrup 144
Strawberry Ricotta Whole Wheat Pancakes 68
Strawberry Syrup 139
Sweet Potato Latkes with Barbecue Pulled Pork
    and Coleslaw 102

T

Tex-Mex Quinoa Cakes 90

W

Whole Wheat Butternut Squash Pancakes 64
Whole Wheat Flaxseed Pancakes 63
Whole Wheat Sweet Potato Oatmeal Pancakes 67

ABOUT THE AUTHOR

Karly is a wife, mother, homeschooler, food blogger, and social media enthusiast. She married her high school sweetheart and has been feeding his cookie addiction ever since.

Karly began cooking frozen pizzas for her young family, progressed to boxed meals somewhere along the way, and finally discarded the boxes and found her groove in the kitchen. Since discovering her love of real homemade food, she has become an avid cook and baker. In late 2008, Karly started the blog *Buns in My Oven*, and she turned it into a full-time venture mid-2012. When Karly isn't homeschooling her kids or binge-watching television series, you'll find her developing recipes for her blog and many national brands.

Buns in My Oven has been featured on many popular websites and was named one of the Top 100 Mom Food Blogs by Disney's *Babble* for 2013, as well as one of the top ten blogs by Huffington Post.

ACKNOWLEDGMENTS

I'd like to thank all of the lovely people who read my blog, *Buns in My Oven*. Without my readers, I wouldn't be here sharing my love of pancakes with all of you. I truly believe that I have the best job out there. I work in my pajamas, I'm paid to eat dinner, and I can justify upgrading my camera equipment as often as possible without eye-rolls from my husband. It's a dream, and I'm so thankful that I'm living it.

Of course, I couldn't do any of this without my hard-working husband. If he weren't so willing to work, work, work, I never would have gotten the chance to be a stay-at-home mom, which means that I never would have found my way to this place. We'd still be eating frozen pizza and canned ravioli for dinner, most likely. Husband, I love you and appreciate everything you've done for this family. Also, you're pretty cute and totally a big deal.

I have to give a big thanks to my sweet children for being more than happy to taste-test every pancake that came off my griddle and for taking the matter seriously. They weren't scared to tell me when a recipe didn't work, and I appreciate every ounce of feedback I received from them. They ate pancakes for breakfast, lunch, and dinner more times than I care to admit, and peanut butter and jelly sandwiches the rest of the time. I promise to start cooking something other than pancakes again now, guys! Thank you, Elijah, for always helping me when asked without a single complaint, and for always keeping an eye on your sister during my many, many runs to the grocery store. Thank you, Emma, for being my little buddy and getting me out of the kitchen for shopping dates and girl time. You two make my world go 'round.

To my parents, thank you for putting up with me, for encouraging me, for believing in me, even when maybe you shouldn't have. I love you both more than I can say.

To my mother-in-law, for being one of my biggest cheerleaders through this journey, thank you. I'm so happy to have you in my life.

And to everyone else, from my Aunt Kimmy to all of my friends (both those I only know online through blogging and those I know "in real life"), who stood by me and cheered me on: I love you, appreciate you, and think you're pretty great.